ZEN
JUDO

ZEN JUDO

A WAY OF LIFE

Brian N. Bagot

4th Dan Zen

Foreword by Dominick McCarthy

7th Dan Zen Judo Family

BLANDFORD

First published in the UK 1989 by
Blandford Press,
An imprint of Cassell,
Artillery House, Artillery Row,
London SW1P 1RT

Distributed in the United States by
Sterling Publishing Co, Inc,
2 Park Avenue, New York NY 10016

Distributed in Australia by
Capricorn Link (Australia) Pty Ltd
PO Box 665, Lane Cove, NSW 2066

British Library Cataloguing in Publication Data
Bagot, Brian N.
  Zen judo : a way of life.
  I. Judo – Manuals
  I. Title
  796.8'152

ISBN 0 7137 2052 2

Typeset by Graphicraft Typesetter Limited

Printed in Great Britain at The Bath Press, Avon

CONTENTS

FOREWORD

Foreword by Dominick McCarthy
7th Dan Zen Judo Family

To Dr Jigoro Kano, founder of this 'Wonderful Way of Life', and all others who followed him and those who still keep his work and name alive today.

As a humble being I try hard to pass on to others his marvellous skill. As the great man said, 'It is for everyone'.

It is not confined to associations and committees. It spells freedom for all people. It eliminates fools who abuse it and allows the dedicated to prevail.

Time is of no consequence. You cannot be in a hurry on a round planet or, to put it nearer home, why hurry when you're not going out of the room in which you are practising.

Love your practice and it will reward you.

My respects to the Amateur Judo Association, the British Judo Association and the British Judo Council.

Dominick Charles McCarthy

AUTHOR'S PREFACE

This book is not about competitive Judo, and the Zen style is not suited to those who wish to carry their physical training to the limit. If you are a player who is looking for clubs where your prowess at *competition* can be stretched, then my advice is not to inflict yourself upon a Zen club, or a Zen club upon yourself. You will only be disappointed, and the club membership will be pleased to see your inevitable departure. If, on the other hand, you are a player searching for a chance to build on your technique or to learn other techniques, then I can only advise you to visit a Zen club and see Zen Judo for yourself.

Zen Judo accepts students of all ages from six to sixty, male or female. Those without preconceived ideas of the art are most suited, and progress quicker, than those with previous experience. Zen Judo is still only in its infancy, but is growing rapidly and will one day rank among the more popular Judo styles. Needless to say Zen Judo is very different in nature to the other styles and possesses a charisma all its own. The Zen club is usually a close-knit organisation enjoying a friendly atmosphere both on and off the mat. This is the reason that the organisation is called the 'Zen Judo Family'.

I sincerely hope that the friendly and caring spirit of the Zen Judo Family has been encapsulated within the pages of this book. You will notice that the text only covers the student's progress during the initial training period up to the grade of 1st Dan. Your progress thereafter will be the subject of a further book in the future dealing with Dan-grade tuition, further techniques and *kata*.

Brian N. Bagot

INTRODUCTION

Zen Judo was founded in 1974 by Dominick McCarthy, a man who has trained in both Judo and Karate for many years. The concept of Zen Judo is a reversion to and a building on the original or traditional style of Judo as pioneered by Dr Jigoro Kano. Since World War Two the Europeans have developed Judo as a sport rather than an art, and the advent of the Olympic Judo competitions has changed the traditional values associated with this art. Nowadays the object of Judo is to win, albeit within the scope of the rules, and gradings in the sport are based primarily upon success in competition.

The traditional Judo values are, to many, far more important than an obsession with winning in all walks of life. In Zen Judo the accent is on achieving perfection of technique in all throws and holds, helping your partner in a search for perfection rather than beating your partner, and achieving a confidence in your ability whereby you feel no need to 'prove yourself' on the mat by resisting all throws put on you by lesser grades.

This is not to say that competition does not play any part in Zen Judo. There are inter-club competitions, team competitions and annual individual events which are run more or less to the European Judo rules which currently prevail. Such competitions have proved as hard as any run by many other Judo associations, and several players have joined Zen from other styles to concentrate upon technique in their search for further knowledge.

I was lucky enough to find myself working near the main headquarters of Zen Judo when I had the time and inclination to try Judo. I feel sure that if I had tried the purely competitive style I would not have continued for very long. The nurturing style of Zen, and the carefully graded structure of its syllabus, ensure that you are introduced to Judo in a prudent and highly controlled manner. The grades are awarded for pure technical knowledge and skill rather than competitive success. This does not mean that grades are given away, rather they are awarded following an arduous grading session under the eye of a competent instructor. The grading sessions become progressively harder and longer as you climb the ladder, whilst the perfection of technique expected at each grading will increase.

My progress through the grades of the Zen Judo Family (a name recently ascribed to the style by Sensei McCarthy) was initially slow, due probably to my age and to the fact that I was by no means a 'natural'. I had to overcome difficulties at almost every stage, and still do to this day, although most difficulties succumb with time and patience. It was with the help of Sensei McCarthy and some of his instructors that I was successful in surmounting the obstacles placed by my mind and body along the way to my black belt. It is because of, rather than in spite of, these problems that I feel competent to write this book.

As a first Kyu (brown belt) I moved to another part of the country, where I started up my own club. The club has grown in strength and popularity over the years and is now among the strongest in the Zen Family. My style of instruction has been tempered by the many setbacks that I have experienced, and readers will note the care with which I try to explain those areas which may become stumbling-blocks for others. All clubs are styled upon their instructors, and although I belong to the Zen Family there are several areas in which I tend to depart from Sensei McCarthy's teaching style.

There has not been a published manual for Zen Judo – only a series of duplicated sheets – and now some thirteen years after its founding I feel that the time has come for a comprehensive text which will serve to introduce newcomers to this alternative form of Judo, and which can also act as a manual for the members of the Zen Judo Family. With this in mind I have endeavoured to depart from the tried and tedious format of other Judo books, and have laid out this manual so that students can see exactly what they need to learn for each grading. Chapters on combination techniques and sacrifice techniques give most of the various requirements of the syllabus and, in addition, I have included some of my methods of instruction where I feel it may be necessary. I make no apology for treating my students with extra care, as I feel that this will be eventually reflected in the amount of understanding between student and instructor in the future.

Zen Judo is an art for everyone. Zen can cater for fighters and thinkers: the fighters learn how to channel their aggression and control it, whilst the others are free to enjoy their Judo without being piled through the mat.

It is my hope that this book will encourage people to join the Zen Family who have hitherto been put off from Judo by the competitive element contained in the European style. It is my belief that Zen Judo has a big future in Britain and elsewhere. There are now Zen clubs starting in the British Army of the Rhine, and my own club is closely associated with the Hemsbach Judo Club in Germany.

Finally it is also my hope that this book will provide coherence once and for all to the Zen Family syllabus. There have been several amendments over the years, and this book itself has precipitated a rethink of the grading syllabus. There has tended to be an accent upon the right-handed techniques in the past. This has now been reconciled by Sensei McCarthy, with the full syllabus to be performed to both right and left.

I wish to thank Sensei McCarthy and his chief instructors for their help in compiling this text. I also wish to thank the members of the Wareham Zen Judo Club who were so patient when I practised all the combinations upon them, and who provided me with ample criticisms of my text during the draft of this book.

1
ETIQUETTE AND RULES OF THE DOJO

The Japanese word *reishiki* means etiquette. The reason that etiquette is stressed as being so important in Judo, and particularly within the Zen Judo Family, is twofold. Firstly, the fundamental philosophy underlying Judo is that its practitioners should live honestly, respectfully and free from outside distractions, involving themselves deeply in Judo, an activity which reaches beyond conscious thought. Through the intricate etiquette required, the Judoka (someone who practises Judo) achieves a tranquillity that is part of his or her manner both within and outside the *Dojo* (practice hall).

Secondly, etiquette is important because it makes the Judoka more capable of self defence. When you as a Judoka observe etiquette until it becomes automatic, you will observe it automatically in any situation calling for your skills. This does not mean that you will bow to an attacker before defending yourself, but it implies that you will not need to think before countering an unprovoked attack upon your person.

Reishiki consists mainly of different forms of bowing (rei), which are performed at certain times. The bow is a sign of salutation or respect within the martial arts world; there are no religious connotations. Donn Draeger, in his book *Modern Bu Jutsu and Budo*, has said, 'personal interests have narrowed the scope of Judo; many of its important cultural aspects have been played down in favour of a few specialised ones'. It is one objective of the Zen Judo Family to ensure that the cultural aspects of Judo are preserved as far as possible.

THE BOW

The bow can be performed either standing or kneeling (*zarei*). A standing bow (*tachirei*) is performed facing the mat or the senior instructor, when either entering or leaving the *dojo* or the mat area. It is also performed before and after *randori* (free practice) or *shiai* (contest). The kneeling bow is only utilised for the start and finish of a training session.

The etiquette for the player who is late entering the *dojo*, after the session has commenced, is that you are expected to step on to the edge of the mat and remain in formal kneeling position (*seiza*) until you are noticed by the senior instructor. When you are invited on to the mat you immediately perform *zarei* before rising to take your place.

Tachirei – The standing bow is performed with feet together and the hands sliding down to your knees. Your eyes should be looking to your front and you must be aware of what is going on around you.

Tachirei – Standing Bow

This is performed with feet together and hands at the side of your hips, fingers extended downwards. Bend forward at the waist, keeping the neck straight and not allowing your head to flop forwards. Your hands extend down the front of your thighs to your knees. This position is held for about half a second, then you return to your original upright posture.

The *tachirei* in a contest situation must be performed with your head in a more upright position, keeping your eyes constantly upon your opponent.

Zarei – Kneeling Bow

This is performed from the formal *seiza* position. From the standing position, extend your left foot backwards and lower the left knee to the mat. Your right knee follows, keeping your hands at your sides. Your feet slide back so that the insteps are flat on the mat, big toes touching one another. Sit back onto your heels, your hands sliding around to the tops of your thighs.

Seiza – This is the formal position for sitting when attending to demonstrations or in preparation for *zarei*, the kneeling bow.

To make *zarei*, slide your hands forward and onto the mat about 4–6 inches in front of your knees, fingers pointing to a spot about 18 inches in front of the centre of your knees. Bend your elbows, lowering your body and head. Always keep your eyes slightly up so that you are aware of what is happening around you. Hold the position for two seconds and then return to *seiza*. When rising, you get up in reverse order from the way you knelt down: right foot first then left, hands returning to your sides.

These forms of bowing are the usual salutations performed on the Judo mat. In other forms of martial arts, different *reishiki* is used and the form of bowing may vary. A supplicant bow is performed in certain styles where the palms of the hands are pressed together in an attitude of prayer as you bow. A strength/peace bow may be performed where the right fist is pressed into the left palm during the bow.

RULES OF THE DOJO

There are certain rules which should be common to all *dojos* throughout the Judo community. These are basically rules of conduct and hygiene, and the latter are necessary to prevent the spread of certain communicable diseases whilst on the mat. The ten basic rules are as follows:

1　Players should always wear some sort of foot covering whilst not on the mat. Straw sandals (*zoris*) are the traditional footwear, but any cheap pair of flip-flops is acceptable. This rule is essential to ensure that the mat surface is kept clean and free from contamination.

2 Players should keep their bodies, especially their feet, scrupulously clean. Players with dirty feet should not be permitted on to the mat. I remember one new player on the mat was a chimney sweep who had not washed properly after his day's work. As he walked over the canvas he left a trail of large, black footprints. Sensei McCarthy spotted this after about four paces, and two large Dan grades were instructed to pick the chap up bodily and carry him to the washroom where his feet were thoroughly cleaned.

3 Players should not wear rings, earrings or any other jewellery, including hair decorations, on the mat. These may become caught up in a suit and the resulting accident could have serious consequences for the wearer.

4 Finger and toe-nails must be kept cut short. Long nails can be very sharp and often cause injury to other players which may lead to secondary infections.

5 Long hair can be dangerous on the mat during contest sessions. Hair should be tied back, pony-tail style, when taking part in contests or heavy *randori*.

6 The wearing of socks on the mat is not to be encouraged. The wearer will be prone to slip on some mat surfaces and may fall badly. Socks should only be permitted when the player is suffering from a foot infection or condition.

7 Players should not wear any top clothing under their Judo suits (*gis*) except in exceptional circumstances. Women and girls may wear T-shirts.

8 Players must *not* leave the mat without the permission of the instructor who is taking the class. When leaving the mat, even for a few seconds, remember to bow as you leave (and when you return), and to don your footwear.

9 Players should not talk whilst seated on the mat during *randori* or contests. Players should sit cross-legged for their own protection and should pay attention to what is happening. If they are out of position and inattentive, they will have little protection if a player is accidentally thrown on to them. This is not to say that a few words spoken quietly to your companion will be penalised.

10 The general posture of the player must be one of attentiveness at all times. To lean against a wall, lounge around or lie down is not permitted. When standing, the arms must hang loosely by your sides. When sitting, your hands should be relaxed and placed upon your knees.

Dan grades are not expected to sit on the mat except if told to by the senior instructor.

This set of rules is common to all *dojos* in the Zen Judo Family, and probably to most other *dojos* where martial arts are practised. There will obviously be some exception to every rule, for instance when a wedding ring cannot be removed. In such circumstances the player should be warned of the possible danger and offered a bandage to cover it. In contest situations such jewellery must be carefully bandaged.

Judo is a potentially dangerous activity, and players should not be distracted by undue noise or movement from the sidelines. A noisy class renders the instructor inaudible and adds to the dangers. The *dojo* is traditionally a place for study and concentration, and all activities in the room should be carried out with this in mind. Modern *dojos* situated in the corners of sports halls or similar do not lend themselves easily to concentration when people next to you are playing badminton or some other sport, but every effort should be made to encourage concentration during the session.

THE BELT

Finally, one small part of martial arts etiquette which is often ignored is the wearing of your belt when visiting other clubs. Japanese etiquette demands that, whatever grade you may be, when you visit another club or style of martial art you present yourself wearing a white belt. The instructor should enquire of you what grade you hold and then may ask you to don your correct belt, thus acknowledging your grade and as a mark of mutual respect.

This aspect of etiquette is rarely seen nowadays, although I have had several visitors appear with white belts over the years, so it is still encouraged in some clubs. Such practices are very much in the tradition of the original martial arts, and should be encouraged to continue.

2
BASICS OF
THROWING TECHNIQUES

As this book is intended for students of the Zen style of Judo, I have presupposed that the readers are already practising Judo at a club of their choice. Thus I have decided not to dwell upon the basics which you are taught on your first visit to a club: the techniques of breakfalling. A description of breakfalling (a technique of falling to avoid injury) would be lengthy and proper coverage of this subject would entail several pages which could be more usefully employed upon other subject matter.

Breakfalls can only be taught properly under the guidance of an experienced player, and a written description could possibly do more harm than good. My advice to all who wish to try the Art is to visit a local Judo club for instruction. If you do not enjoy the club, do not give up but visit another one, because no two clubs are run the same way and each will have a different slant upon the Art.

Because Zen Judo is striving towards perfection of technique, the throws utilised in the syllabus must be performed in the correct manner. Each standing technique can be broken down into three elements: moving into the throw, the throw itself, and your posture afterwards. There are other ways of breaking down throwing techniques, but I have chosen this method as it can be used to illustrate certain basics which are vital in the early stages of your training.

Learning the throw itself is an essential part of all training, and the way that each throw is entered is described in chapter three. In this chapter, however, I shall look in greater detail at each of the three elements of the throw. It is in the method of entry that many beginners pick up certain faults which may be difficult to rectify later on; however, the main accent of this chapter will be on posture during and after the throw, as this makes the difference between a good throw and a scrappy one which is visually ugly and which will probably be most uncomfortable for your partner to breakfall from.

The Japanese terms of Tori and Uke are used extensively in the diagrams and text in this chapter. Tori is the player who performs the throw, Uke the player who gets thrown.

Japanese terms used in the book can be found at the end in the glossary of terms.

METHOD OF ENTRY

With hip throws there are essentially three methods of entry which can be utilised. These are as follows:

Two Steps

Turn your body to your left, place your right foot just inside Uke's right foot, toes pointing away from Uke. Bring your left foot back and inside Uke's left foot, toes pointing away from Uke. This sequence is shown diagrammatically:

Method of entry – Two steps

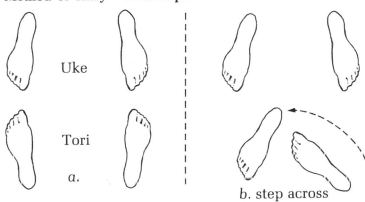

a.

b. step across

c. pivot round left foot

This movement may be extended for such throws as *tai otoshi, uki goshi ashi guruma* and *harai goshi*, but all utilise the same basic format. Alternative methods of entry, although not impossible to adapt for these throws, may leave you off balance and vulnerable. It is therefore essential that this is the basic method of entry taught to all beginners.

The Pivot

This is a quick method of entry for some hip techniques which lends itself to the competition situation. Unfortunately some players can get themselves into the habit very early in their Judo careers of entering in this fashion for all throws, and they meet with difficulties later when retraining out of this habit. This entry cannot be used for throws such as *ashi* and *o guruma, koshi guruma, ko tsuri goshi* or *hane goshi*, but inexperienced students tend to think that the pivot entry can be adapted for all techniques. Instructors should only teach this entry when the student is thoroughly familiar with the two-step entry.

The pivot utilises a step across Uke and a pivot around your left foot:

The Pivot

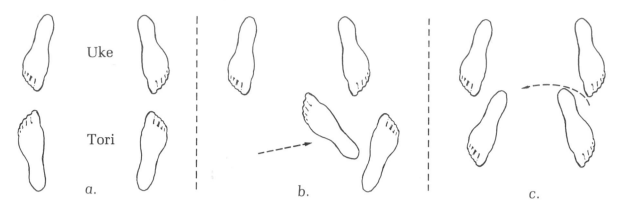

a.   *b.*   *c.*

The Back Step

This is the entry for the competition style where speed is essential and must be coupled with a powerful and low stance. Enter by pivoting on your right foot, bringing your left foot back and outside Uke, then extend your right foot across Uke's ankles:

The back step

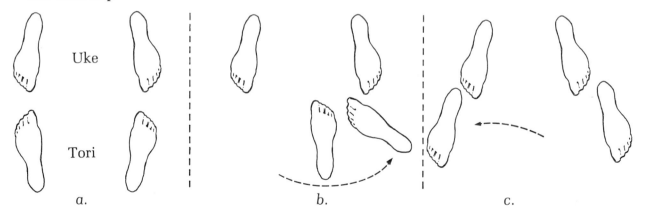

a.   *b.*   *c.*

HANDS AND ARMS

There are two positions for the right hand/arm in a right-handed throw. You may either keep your grip on Uke's collar in the front or to the top of the suit, or you may let go, sliding your arm around Uke's neck or waist. When Uke is taller than yourself it is best to slide your arm around Uke's back, under the left armpit. In Zen Judo the demonstration of formal standing techniques usually necessitates your right arm encircling Uke's neck. This tends to pull Uke nearer to Tori, thus facilitating the throw.

In *randori* or *shiai* there is no time to put your arm round Uke's neck or waist, and the act of sliding your arm around your opponent's neck leaves you vulnerable to certain techniques. Your right hand therefore remains gripping Uke's left lapel.

For grading at higher levels the throws are expected to be performed from three hand positions: round the neck, on collar and sleeve, and under the arm. There are of course some throws which do not lend themselves to more than one or two of these positions.

The right arm which encircles the neck is for guidance only and it should not be utilised for the purposes of throwing. The throw is executed by pulling upon Uke's right sleeve with your left hand, and turning your body to the left as you wind in for the throw. There is nothing more uncomfortable than having to practise with a new student who continually grasps you round the neck, endeavouring to pull your head off in his or her effort to produce *tai otoshi* or *kubi nage*. This fault should be corrected at the beginning of the student's career.

POSTURE WHILST THROWING

The elements of clean throwing do not stop at the bodily extremities. The whole of your body must be utilised every time you perform a throw, and instruction should be given in these elements to all beginners.

Knees

Your knees are the shock absorbers for your body. A stiff-legged person is quite easy to unbalance, whilst a person standing with feet apart and knees slightly bent is very difficult to unbalance. It is thus essential that the Judo player always keeps his or her knees slightly bent so as to readily absorb the actions of other players.

Feet

The placing of your feet is important, and the closer together they are the more unbalanced your posture becomes. When moving around the mat your feet should brush the surface lightly. The most powerful position for your feet is either side of your shoulders, knees bent, and it is in this position that you are expected to complete your throwing technique.

Back

The player who continually bends forward in order not to be thrown is vulnerable to an experienced player. Some throws require you to bend forwards in their execution, such as *kata seoi*, *seoi nage* and *o goshi*; however the majority should be performed with a more upright stance. The correct posture when throwing is to have a straight back with shoulders level, knees slightly bent and feet placed at right angles to one another and slightly wider than the shoulders.

FINISHING THE THROW

There are many ways of finishing a throw, probably as many ways as there are throws, and many players can be seen to end up sitting or sprawling on the mat, even when they are Tori, after a throw. It is vital to maintain your balance at all times, especially when you have just thrown Uke as this is the moment when you can be vulnerable — the point of the sacrifice counter.

If you are bent forward over Uke, it is a simple matter to be pulled over and on to the ground as Uke rolls over. The two points to bear in mind are, firstly, that you must maintain good balance and, secondly, that you should aid Uke to breakfall.

The posture to aim for at the termination of your throw is to have your feet wide apart and at 90 degrees to one another, knees slightly bent and back straight. You should be holding Uke's right sleeve with your left hand, pulling upwards slightly to aid breakfall. Your right hand should fall naturally to Uke's right wrist. From this position you are able to progress to *newaza* (groundholds) or *atemi* (hitting or punching) with fist, elbow or foot depending on the situation. The correct posture from a hand or hip throw is shown below.

Posture – The correct position following a throw is with the knees bent, back straight and your right hand in a controlling position. Note the breakfall position with left arm close to Uke's side and the body relaxed.

The slight lift of Uke's right arm is important to aid break-fall, and should be practised by all beginners so that it becomes a natural part of their throwing action. Many players are capable of throwing their partners very hard, and to land flat on your back from a well-timed throw can be a memorable experience which you will not wish to repeat.

One of the objectives of Zen Judo is to help your partner also to improve, and it follows that you should treat your partner in the same manner as you yourself would wish to be treated. To deliberately throw over-hard is to begin a succession of competing throws which may well lead to bruising or injury, and resultant bad feeling between players. Sensei McCarthy has often been heard to admonish players who exhibit the slightest animosity on his mat, and this should be the case throughout the Zen Family clubs.

Finally, and equally as important, is the position that Uke lands in on the mat. From a right-hand throw Uke should finish up in left breakfall approximately 180 degrees from the starting-point. This, of course, does not hold true for every throw in the syllabus, for example *ko tsuri goshi*, *koshi guruma*, *hane goshi* and several others.

Landing on the mat

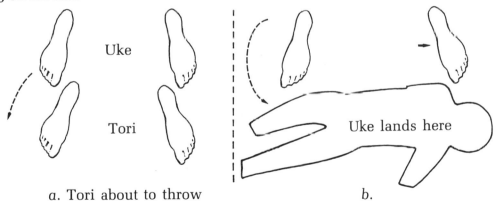

a. Tori about to throw   b.

Uke

Tori

Uke lands here

This chapter has been devoted to breaking down the basic throwing technique into its component parts, considering each of these individually and trying to offer advice as to how to perfect your technique. The throws this chapter is mainly concerned with are the hand, hip and foot throws which involve turning in rather than stepping forward.

The possibility of *atemi*, a blow to a vital spot, has been mentioned. This will be elaborated upon in chapter nine on *atemiwaza*. The objective of this chapter is to enable you to position yourself correctly to deliver *atemi* if the situation demands it.

3
THE ZEN SYLLABUS
OF STANDING TECHNIQUES

The majority of manuals on Judo find it satisfactory just to list up to forty of the more well-known throws, giving little indication of the stage at which they will be introduced. In the case of Zen Judo, the order in which the throws appear is vital to the preparation of the student for each grading. These stages are very carefully controlled, and new throws are not usually taught until the student successfully passes the next belt grading.

It must be emphasised again that success in grading is *not* based on prowess in competition, but on the student's knowledge and perfection of the techniques. The throws listed in the sections of this chapter form only the start of each grading syllabus. Not only will the student be expected to know the required throws, and those from all previous gradings, but to apply them in both right- and left-hand form to counter techniques, combination techniques and sacrifice/half sacrifice techniques. Only the throws will be described in this chapter. For descriptions of combination techniques, counters, hold-downs and other techniques you will need to consult later chapters.

This chapter, which naturally forms the bulk of this book, is broken down into separate sections, each dealing with a specific grading (for example yellow to orange belt). The details of each grading are listed in appendix A. Remember, each grading includes *all* techniques from the previous gradings, so the gradings become longer as you progress up through the belts.

Gradings may be carried out within each individual Zen club up to the grade of orange belt. After that stage the higher gradings are currently held in the headquarters *dojo* at four-monthly intervals. These grading sessions usually take place on the first Sunday in the months of March, July and November. They are held behind closed doors where the public cannot view the proceedings and the students cannot be distracted. I think that the first of these gradings is probably the most nerve-racking, as you do not know what to expect. So long as the student knows the syllabus there should be little to worry about. Forgetting one or two throws in the session is no great sin; however, a lack of knowledge of a complete section of the syllabus (for example technique threes or counter twos) will probably lead to failure.

In all gradings the examiner is not seeking for an excuse to fail the candidate, but trying to pass him or her. It is just as difficult for an examiner to tell a student that he or she has failed the grading after a couple of hours of hard work as it is for the student to go through a tough grading session. I have experienced both sides of the fence and understand the feeling of failure. The only consolation is that a second try after four months usually results in success.

My only advice to the novice who is hoping to one day qualify for a black belt with the Zen Judo Family is to sit back and enjoy the years of training. Training too hard or too seriously will not lead to enjoyment of your belt, whatever colour it may be, and your attitude towards Judo is taken into account during the brown and black belt gradings. The student who will achieve most from training is one who remains cheerful at all times and provides a great deal of help to the lower grades. After orange belt you are sometimes called upon to teach lower grades, especially juniors, and this is the main testing ground for your potential as black belts. If you can enjoy the training and the opportunity to train others, you are on the right road to success.

WHITE TO YELLOW BELT

Only four throws are included at this initial stage. Each throw forms the basis of many other techniques that you will learn as you progress in Zen Judo. *Kubi nage*, for instance, forms the basis of many techniques including *ko tsuri goshi*, *hiki tai*, *seoi nage* and *o goshi*. Each of the four throws utilises a different foot placing and basic movement, so that the beginner receives a firm foundation upon which to build.

KUBI NAGE

This is probably the simplest and most basic of throws which involves Tori turning in. This technique as it stands would rarely be used during *randori* or contests because of its simplicity, and the fact that it is not a 'strong' technique. It is easy to spoil or counter, and relies for its execution upon speed and a certain naïveté on Uke's part.

Turn in so that your feet are inside Uke's feet and your back to Uke's chest. Your right arm slides across Uke's shoulders and around the neck, bringing Uke's head forward under your right arm. A pull on Uke's sleeve with your left hand

and a turn of your hips to the left will complete the throw.

Although a simple throw, it is of great importance to be able to execute *kubi nage* properly as this technique is the basis of many other throws you will meet. In gradings, the student is expected to know the basic techniques, and mistakes in such throws as *kubi nage* will not be tolerated for long.

ASHI GAKE

Again, this is the basic throw to the rear which relies upon your breaking Uke's balance to the rear and continuing the movement until Uke has fallen. This throw, because of its simplicity, has little use in competition, but is used to teach the method of entry for harder throws such as *o soto guruma*.

Step forward with your left foot, in line with and outside Uke's right foot. Your right hand is brought over Uke's left shoulder and forces Uke backwards and downwards. Your right foot is passed between your left leg and Uke's right leg to block behind Uke's right ankle. A second step forward with your left foot completes the throw.

Ashi gake – Tori is in the correction position with her right leg well between Uke's legs, right hand over Uke's shoulder and about to step forward with her left leg.

Ashi gake

It is important to ensure that the initial step forward with your left foot is taken to the side of Uke's foot or further forward. If not brought far enough forward it will unbalance you to your rear and the throw will not succeed. The right foot must be brought round Uke's right ankle and placed on the mat deeply between Uke's legs prior to stepping forward again.

KO UCHI MAKI KOMI

This movement introduces the principle of the inside winding or blocking throws, such as *uchi ashi sasae* or *ko uchi gari*. It is only a simple block to one leg and a push back which would not work in a contest situation, but it is the basic movement that is being learned rather than a hard throw for use on the mat. It can serve as a different and useful counter *to hiza guruma* if used quickly and precisely.

Put your right hand on Uke's left shoulder, pushing to the rear. Slide your right foot between Uke's legs and block Uke's right heel from the rear. Your left hand drops to Uke's knee, thumb downwards, to hold the lower leg in place and stop Uke from stepping back with that foot. Lean forwards on to Uke to unbalance him or her backwards and complete the throw.

Ko uchi maki komi

The throw should be executed in a single flowing motion rather than in three separate phases as appears to be indicated by the text. All hand and foot movements are performed virtually simultaneously for the throw to be effective. As you progress up the belts, so this action will develop and form the basis for many other throws.

TAI OTOSHI

This is the only throw within this first syllabus which you will still be using regularly when you become a black belt. *Tai otoshi* is a firm favourite with all Judo players because of its basic simplicity and potential effectiveness. There are many variations of the throw in use but I will only describe two of these. The first version is the way it is taught initially to beginners in Zen Judo, whilst the second is the more competitive version which is introduced at a later stage. If you try out both methods when you are on the mat, you will notice a great difference in the force with which Uke is thrown.

(a) Step in as for *kubi nage*, right arm around Uke's neck. Now step across Uke's right leg with your right foot, blocking the ankle. Pull Uke's right sleeve across your chest with your left hand, turning your body to your left to ease Uke round your hip and complete the throw.

Tai otoshi

Tai otoshi – This is the version as taught to the beginner with your arm around Uke's neck.

Tai otoshi – This is the more advanced version performed without moving your hands from Uke's collar or sleeve. Note that a lower stance is adopted for this version.

(b) Step back and round your right foot with your left foot so that it points in the same direction as Uke's left foot but outside it. Step across with your right foot to outside Uke's right foot. Keep turning to your left pulling Uke's sleeve with your left hand and his or her collar with your right hand to complete the throw.

TECHNIQUE TWOS

Combination techniques within this syllabus are simple, and the usual combinations expected are:

(1) *kubi nage/tai otoshi* or *kubi nage/ko uchi maki komi*;
(2) *ashi gake/tai otoshi* or *ashi gake/ko uchi maki komi*;
(3) *ko uchi maki komi/kubi nage* or *ko uchi maki komi/ ashi gake*;
(4) *tai otoshi/kubi nage* or *tai otoshi/ko uchi maki komi*.

For white belts an interesting combination is to teach a technique four using all these throws: *ashi gake/tao otoshi/ kubi nage/ko uchi maki komi*. You can, of course, start with any of these throws to achieve a viable technique four.

COUNTERS

The simple counter one technique is described in the appropriate chapter later on, and is used for each of these throws. The only difficulty seems to be with *ashi gake* which, if allowed to go on too far, can be virtually impossible to effectively counter in this manner. The counter should be applied early and quickly.

GROUNDHOLDS

Kesa gatame and *kazure kesa gatame* are stipulated for this grading. These are described in the chapter on hold-downs.

The final part of the grading is the performance of *randori*, usually at the end of the instruction session. During your turn it is expected that you try to use each of your throws to the right and to the left, and combination techniques and counters where possible. During a grading *randori* session the senior belt should be co-operative and allow you to demonstrate your knowledge of your syllabus without the distraction of fighting too hard to apply the throws.

When you are finally awarded your belt you will be called to the centre of the mat, knelt on one knee and asked to remove your white belt. The yellow belt is presented to you and you are asked to put it on. Whilst you are doing this the instructor should talk quietly to you about your future conduct on the mat and stress that you respect those grades lower than yourself. With your belt finally in place you both stand. You bow to the instructor and take your place at the end of the line of yellow belts before the session finishes. This short ceremony takes place for all yellow and orange gradings.

In conclusion, remember that as a yellow belt you have shown not only that can you perform your *kihon* (basic throws), but also that you can be thrown. This means that senior grades will start to throw you a little harder during *randori* and will expect you to be able to breakfall correctly most times. Make an effort to relax and try to practise your breakfalls during each instruction session when you are being thrown.

YELLOW TO ORANGE BELT

The throws in this section have been carefully chosen so that you will now feel that you are really beginning to be thrown. In some techniques you are lifted on to your toes (*kata seoi; obi goshi*) so that your footwork is disrupted, but generally the techniques are gentle and flexible. Note, though, that most of the techniques are capable of being used as good hip throws at a later stage, even though the yellow belts are only encouraged to pull Uke around their hips rather than over them.

The accent in this syllabus is on turning in, progressive use of the hips, and footwork. When you are able to turn in properly for hip and shoulder throws, and are thoroughly familiar with the syllabus of combination and counter throws, you will be in a position to continue ahead with the next grading.

KATA SEOI

In many Judo manuals this technique is referred to as *ippon seoi nage*. However, as it is the shoulder throw featured in formal Judo demonstrations (*kata*), it has been designated as *kata seoi*. There is a lot of flexibility in *kata seoi* and it can be developed into quite a hard technique as you progress. At this stage, however, it is taught as a gentle shoulder throw in which Uke is pulled around your hip.

You step in with your right foot then your left, bringing your feet inside Uke's feet as in *kubi nage*. Your right arm is thrust under Uke's right armpit, pulling Uke's right sleeve across your chest with your left hand. Turn to your left and throw Uke around your right shoulder. The throw can, of course, be augmented by putting your hip through and into Uke to make the throw higher and harder. This will be practised once you are preparing for your next grading.

Kata seoi – This shoulder throw is performed by partially lifting Uke with your right shoulder and turning to your left.

Kata seoi

RYO ASHI DORI

This throw is referred to as *morote gari* in some styles where a violent sweeping action with the hands is used. In *ryo ashi dori* the hands are used to block only, the impetus for the throw coming from Tori's shoulders leaning on to Uke and pushing him or her backwards.

You squat down in front of Uke with your right leg across Uke's lower legs. Pass your right hand inside Uke's legs with thumb pointing downwards, and block the left ankle. Pass your left hand, thumb up, around the outside of Uke's right leg to block the right ankle. Lean on to Uke to complete the throw, but do *not* pull Uke's ankles from under him or her.

This appears to be a favourite throw with the smaller children who start Judo, but they should be discouraged from trying it too often.

HIZA GURUMA

Hiza guruma is a foot technique which can be quite spectacular when applied correctly. Again this throw has a built-in flexibility and can be applied quite lightly in the beginning. The application of your foot to Uke's knee should be carried out carefully without force or you will inflict painful bruising or injury.

As in all throws, break Uke's balance forwards with a pull by both hands. Step back towards your right rear corner with your right foot whilst placing the sole of your left foot on the outside of Uke's right knee. Turn your body to the left and wheel Uke over your foot. Your right hand should move in an upward circular direction whilst your left hand moves in a downward direction around the same circle.

Properly executed, Uke will land behind your original position and not to your left side as is too often the case. You should always remember to keep hold of Uke's right sleeve to ease the breakfall and enable you to either enter groundwork or to finish the technique with *atemi*.

Hiza guruma – This knee wheel is performed by Tori pulling Uke over his outstretched foot. Note that Tori has broken Uke's balance to his right front corner to apply the throw.

UKI GOSHI

The translation 'floating hip' is very descriptive of this technique when performed correctly. Unfortunately many players tend to use it as an excuse to perform a bad *o goshi* or *kata nage* and the throw has then become degraded. There should be *no* lifting in *uki goshi*, Uke being drifted around your hip as you complete the turn.

Step in with your right foot to a point midway between Uke's feet, turning so that your right side is against Uke's chest and stomach. Slide your right hand around Uke's waist and across the back. Uke is now thrown by completing your turn, bringing your left foot back outside and in line with your right foot.

The usual fault is that Tori turns completely in with both feet before taking Uke around the hip. This means that an excess of strength is being used to complete the throw and pull Uke around your body. Properly performed, the throw requires little or no strength to complete.

Uki goshi

OBI GOSHI

This throw may be encountered under the name of *tsuri goshi* (lifting hip). It is the first technique in which you are using an item of Uke's clothing to help you lift in order to complete the throw, in this case Uke's belt at the rear. Initially the throw should show lift in that Uke's heels must leave the mat as the throw is entered. As the beginner becomes more experienced, so the hip can be turned in further and the lift will become greater.

You step as in *kubi nage*, your right hand sliding around Uke's waist to grasp the belt (*obi*) at the rear. Turn your hip into Uke's stomach and lift slightly with your right hand, pulling Uke's right sleeve across your chest. Uke will be thrown partly over your hip to land in front of you.

Having brought Uke over your hip, it is important to remember to let go of the belt so that Uke may breakfall properly. Maintain your grip on Uke's right sleeve to ensure a correct breakfall.

ERI NAGE

In this technique you are moving your left-hand grip as well as your right. Again this is a throw which can build up to a good hip throw; however, it is rather slow and cumbersome. This technique may be seen as an intermediate step between *kubi nage* and *seoi nage*, the latter being a fast and effective throw which occurs in your next syllabus.

With your left hand grip Uke's right lapel high up. Slide your right hand down Uke's left lapel to a position lower than that of your left hand. Turn in as for *kubi nage*, folding your right arm so that the forearm is under your left wrist. Lift and turn to complete the throw.

Uke should initially be brought around your hip, not over it. Later on Uke may be lifted partly over the hip, although this technique is not meant to be a major hip throw.

O SOTO GURUMA

This technique has many variations, but at its most basic it comprises breaking Uke's balance backwards, blocking both legs and throwing. It is not a popular throw in contests as you must be in the right position to execute it and an experienced player would not allow you to get that far. Three separate methods are taught within the Zen syllabus, but be aware that other techniques exist bearing the same name. The first method is taught to newcomers to the grade. The second is taught later as they begin to progress, and the third method, which incidentally is the classical throw, is taught when the student is ready for the next belt up.

(a) Step forward with your left foot as in *ashi gake*, but pass your right leg behind both of Uke's legs to a point outside the rear of Uke's left foot. Transfer your weight to your right foot and throw Uke over your outstretched leg diagonally to your right.

(b) Step forward as above, stretching your right leg across the rear of Uke's legs and placing your foot outside Uke's left heel. Pull Uke's right sleeve with your left hand across your body, turning slightly to your left as you throw Uke over your right leg. Throw Uke around to your front to land across your feet.

(c) Step forward as before, breaking Uke's balance to the rear. Swing your right leg through and behind Uke's legs to block them at the the rear. Your right foot should be to the rear of Uke's knee and *not* on the mat. Throw Uke directly backwards with a forward movement of your hips, stepping forwards with your right foot as Uke falls.

O soto guruma

TE HIZA SASAE

The final throw in the syllabus demonstrates the use of your hand to block Uke's progress forward, in order to throw. This technique has two methods of execution, called respectively the 'short' and the 'long' methods. In the short method it is your right shoulder which provides the push to complete the throw, whilst in the long method it is your subsequent step forward which does this.

Te hiza sasae – The propping hand is placed on Uke's knee whilst Tori pulls and turns to the left.

Te hiza sasae – The long version of this throw entails Tori stepping away from Uke whilst blocking with the hand.

31

(a) Turn in as in *kubi nage*, your right hand sliding down Uke's body to block the right knee at the front. Holding Uke's sleeve tightly turn your body to the left so that the leverage of your right shoulder helps to complete the throw.

(b) From the position where you have turned in and blocked with your right hand, step forward with your left foot. The forward movement will pull Uke over your blocking hand to complete the throw. As you progress your block and step will occur simultaneously as shown.

OSAEKOMIWAZA

Four holds are required, two which were performed for the previous grading and two new ones. These are shown in the chapter on groundholds.

COMBINATION TECHNIQUES

Technique threes to each technique are quite viable with the repertoire that you now possess. Bear in mind that the transfer of your hand from Uke's neck to arm or waist will lose you marks in the grading. Also note that technique threes are required to be performed to the left as well as to the right. If your knowledge of the syllabus is thorough, this will be no problem to you.

The main problem is performing technique threes to the simple throws such as *kubi nage*, *ko uchi maki komi*, *tai otoshi*, and so on, because your hand position around the neck must remain there. There are no neck throws in your present syllabus, so you are left with such combinations as *kubi nage/tai otoshi/ko uchi maki komi*.

COUNTERS

Counter ones and twos are required for each throw, and counter ones will be required to both right and left sides.

THROWS TO GROUNDHOLD

Whilst it is comparatively easy to throw Uke and fall naturally into *kesa gatame*, a variety of groundholds is expected at this point in the grading. Although only four holds are taught, all should be demonstrated at this stage.

SHIAI

This is the first grading in which *shiai* (contest) is featured. Although the object of contests is to win, you will not fail the grading if you lose. It is the demonstration of fighting spirit which is expected, and so long as you try hard you will get good marks.

ORANGE TO GREEN BELT

The throws in this section have been carefully selected so that the student's balance can be improved. There are two throws which rely upon good lateral balance, *ashi* and *o guruma*, and another two which require good frontal balance, *ko tsuri goshi* and *koshi guruma*. As Uke, on the other hand, you will find that your feet will leave the mat with regularity, and you must rely therefore upon your ability to breakfall properly.

Another introduction at this stage is the half-sacrifice technique which is performed on one knee, adding greater speed and impetus to your technique. Only four techniques are specified for the grading. However, it must be noted that any of the techniques in the syllabus may be required to be performed with a half-sacrifice if the grader so wishes.

As you will notice, the grading syllabus is beginning to put more accent upon the left-hand techniques. A good all-round player can perform techniques to either side, although the majority will stick to one side or the other, whichever comes most naturally.

KATA NAGE

This technique may be commenced quite lightly to be built up later to a good hip throw, depending upon the placement of your hip. It appears to be a throw which is little used today, most opting for *obi goshi* or *o goshi* which are easier to perform in *randori*.

You turn in as for *kubi nage*, sliding your right arm under Uke's left armpit. Bring your right arm up and bend it so that your hand is pointing forwards over the top of Uke's left shoulder. Keeping your back to Uke and pulling the right sleeve across your chest, turn to your left and throw Uke round your hip. As you gain in skill you will throw Uke over the hip.

ASHI GURUMA

This is the first of the lateral balance throws and it must be entered correctly or it will be difficult to complete. The technique relies upon your pulling Uke close to you as you lift Uke's weight slightly on to your hip to complete the throw.

Kata nage

33

Step back and around with your left foot, placing it on a line drawn through Uke's feet, toes pointing in the same direction as Uke's but on the outside of Uke's left foot. As you turn, pass your right hand well around Uke's neck (or under the arm if Uke is taller than you). Hold Uke tightly to your right side and sway your balance over your left foot, raising your right leg so that your calf is just under Uke's right knee. Uke's weight should be mainly upon your hip. Pull with your left hand and twist your hips to the left as you raise Uke and throw him or her over your outstretched leg.

It is important to maintain full control over Uke during this technique as you may need to augment Uke's breakfall with a pull on the right sleeve. Try to avoid the temptation to sweep your right leg backwards as this negates the technique and the throw will become something else.

Ashi guruma – Uke's weight should be on Tori's hip and the left foot placed outside Uke's left foot. Tori's right foot is lifted only six inches off the mat.

Seoi nage

(MOROTE) SEOI NAGE

This is one of the more popular throws in use today. I personally do not find it easy to perform, but it enjoys an impressive contest record. Uke can be brought gently around your hip at first and you can build up to a full hip throw when confidence is gained.

Turn in as for *kubi nage*, keeping hold of Uke's left lapel with your right hand. Fold your right arm so that the forearm is brought up under Uke's right armpit as you execute the throw. Pull Uke's right sleeve across your chest with your left hand and turn your hip in as you throw.

There is inherently a great amount of control over Uke in this technique as you have good purchase with both hands and you can control Uke's landing as you wish. Retain your hold on the lapel for as long as possible during the throw.

SASAE TSURI KOMI ASHI

Although the beginner may think that this technique is similar to *hiza guruma*, this is far from the case. Their similarity ends in the entry address, as the mechanics behind each are very different. *Hiza guruma* is a wheel throw whilst this technique is primarily a block followed by a lift-pull.

Sasae tsuri komi ashi – Tori's weight is used to augment this technique. Note how Uke's balance is broken to the front.

You take a short step diagonally to your right rear with your right foot. With both hands lift Uke and pull towards you to unbalance Uke to the front. Before he or she can step forward, apply the sole of your left foot to the front of Uke's right shin just above the instep. Lean your weight back and turn away from Uke, pulling Uke over your outstretched foot. Continue turning and lift slightly as Uke falls to ensure correct breakfall.

For the throw to work correctly you must commit yourself completely to the technique. Your lean back must be such that you would fall over if you were not holding Uke. As you turn you regain your balance and come round to the correct posture as Uke breakfalls. Uke should fall across your feet which have turned 180 degrees during the throw. If Uke falls to your left side you have not executed the throw correctly.

O GURUMA

This is a higher and more powerful throw similar to *ashi guruma*. It is very often difficult for the student to raise his or her leg to the required height to execute this technique, especially with Uke spread along the raised leg. The grader will usually make allowances when Uke is obviously heavier than you, or taller, and you experience difficulty in raising the

O guruma

O guruma – Tori's left foot must be outside Uke's left and Tori's right leg raised as high as possible.

weight. Similarly with children who lack the muscular development, allowances will be made. In such cases you must show that you are familiar with the technique by lifting your leg in front of Uke to the correct height, then lowering it to perform *ashi guruma*.

You enter for this throw as in *ashi guruma*, your left foot being placed in line with Uke's feet and well outside his or her left foot. Pass your right arm well around Uke's neck (or back if Uke is taller than you), pulling Uke close to your right side and on to your right hip. Stretch your right leg across the front of Uke's legs. Swing your right leg up, taking the weight of Uke onto your right hip and left leg, lifting Uke off the mat to throw him or her over your outstretched leg.

If you experience problems performing *ashi guruma*, they will be magnified in this throw. It is essential to ensure that Uke's weight is carried on your hip to make the lift easier. You must have extremely close contact with Uke as any gap between you will negate the throw.

KO SOTO GAKE

This is a delicate and difficult throw to perform unless your balance is perfect. You will find initially that your feet tend to come too close together, thus reducing your balance, and a slight error would make you vulnerable. The theory is that you are stepping forward and commencing your turn to your left, as if you were about to enter for a hip throw. Uke begins to resist to the rear and you then enter for the technique, directing Uke backwards in the line of the initial resistance.

With your right foot, step to a point midway between Uke's legs. You may commence a turn to the left at this stage but do not continue it through. Step with your left foot outside Uke's right leg and place your heel to the back of Uke's ankle, your toes on the mat. As you do this, slide your right hand under Uke's left armpit and pull towards your left rear corner. When your foot is in place and Uke begins to resist backwards from your pull, lean forwards and pull down with your left hand on Uke's sleeve to complete the throw.

You must ensure that your first step forwards is not too deep or your balance will become vulnerable. There should ideally be a 15-inch gap between your feet as you perform this technique, thus maintaining your balance.

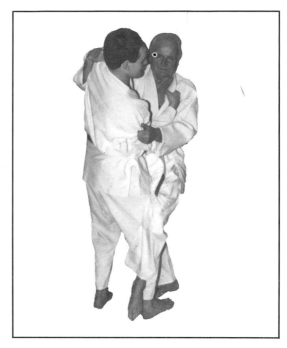

Ko soto gake – Tori's left heel must complete a definite block to Uke's right leg. Note Tori's right arm under Uke's left shoulder.

KO TSURI GOSHI

With this technique and that following, you require good balance in a forward direction, as your feet are placed in line with one another. The impetus for the throw is provided by your hip which lifts Uke off the mat as you perform the technique, hence its name, 'minor lifting hip'.

To turn in you must pivot on the ball of your left foot, sliding your arm well over Uke's shoulder. Your right leg slides back between Uke's legs extending as far as possible to your rear, your toes on the mat and heel raised. Lower your hip and pull Uke down with you, putting tension on the right sleeve with your left hand. The throw may now be completed by *either*:

(a) pulling with your left hand whilst raising your hip to lift Uke off the mat and over your hip; or
(b) pulling with your left hand whilst stepping forward with your right leg and keeping your body low. This draws Uke across your hips by your forward movement.

KOSHI GURUMA

Similarly, this technique requires precise balance akin to the previous technique, only your right leg extends back outside Uke rather than between the legs. It is important in this technique to pull with your left hand and lift at the

Koshi guruma

Koshi guruma – Tori's arm around Uke's neck serves to pull Uke down whilst Tori's right leg is extended back. Note the position of Tori's feet, toes and right knee.

completion to avoid Uke falling flat on to his or her back. This throw tends to knock the breath out of students when first practised. After a while confidence grows and the technique is completed properly and with more comfort to Uke.

Turn in as for *ko tsuri goshi*, sliding your right arm around Uke's neck and across the shoulder. Pivot on the ball of your left foot, swinging your right leg around and deep outside Uke's legs with your right knee very low to the mat. Pull Uke close to you and lift your hip, raising Uke off the mat and over the hip. The walk-out version of this throw may work equally as well for many students, depending on the relative sizes of Uke and Tori.

The most important element in this technique is to ensure that your right knee is lowered almost to the mat. If it is too high it will block Uke's knee and can cause injury, as well as preventing you from raising your hip to complete the throw. In some of our clubs this throw (and that previous) is taught without the lift of the hips, which makes it more difficult to perform. However, there is no difference in the designation of the technique whichever method is taught.

One of the main reasons that this and subsequent gradings are undertaken at the headquarters, and not at your normal instruction sessions, is the length of time required to complete the grading properly. Orange to green gradings can extend for well over two hours at times, much longer than your normal session. Another important point is that you will now be graded by an instructor you are unlikely to know, from another club. It can often be very difficult for your chief instructor to grade you objectively, as he or she will know how you perform normally on the mat and may make excessive allowances for nerves on the day.

This first grading away from your normal surroundings is always nerve-racking, but after the first half-hour of the grading you will tend to forget all about nerves as the concentration required is quite extensive and time passes very quickly. Just try to relax and get on with it – let the grading take care of itself.

GREEN TO BLUE BELT

The syllabus that the newly qualified green belt is introduced to contains much new material. Of these new moves, the sacrifice techniques are the most important, and much time is necessary to practise these throws. It is expected that most students will take, on average, six months between green and blue belts, and this time is taken up with perfecting the new techniques and practising sacrificial techniques in *randori*.

It is at this point that you begin to realise the reasons why your early training contained certain exercises, such as rolling breakfalls over lines of students, which you did not seem to require on the mat. The period is used to help build up confidence in the performance of *sutemiwaza* (techniques whereby Tori sacrifices his or her own posture), and green belt students demonstrate readiness for the next grading when they are taking and performing *sutemi* naturally during *randori*.

Students will note that all sacrifice techniques and counters are to be performed to both right and left. These techniques are usually taught only on the right side, and instructors should take care to ensure that they give sufficient consideration to left-hand techniques at this stage.

O SOTO OTOSHI

This is not a widely practised throw, but it makes a very good lead up to *o soto gari* which appears in the next syllabus. This throw is also an excellent counter to certain rear throws if timed correctly. It must be remembered that the point of contact giving impetus for the technique is the inside of Tori's right thigh against Uke's right thigh.

Step with your left foot outside Uke's right foot, as in *ashi gake*. Pass your right leg around the back of Uke's right leg and deep between them. Drive your foot downwards, straightening your knee, simultaneously pushing backwards and down with your right hand whilst pulling Uke towards

O soto otoshi

you with your left hand. The contact between your thighs will sweep Uke's leg forwards and Uke will land across your feet.

One of the main faults demonstrated by students is a lack of impetus from the thigh contact. The technique will then become indistinguishable from *ashi gake*. Uke should land across you rather than straight backwards, and the final drive of your left foot should precipitate the throw.

TSURI KOMI GOSHI

This is a very difficult technique to perform correctly as it involves a fine balance between strength and posture. It is ideal for a small Tori to perform upon a taller Uke, rather than vice versa. Ideally Uke should be lifted by the upward extension of your right arm. However, this is not that simple, and the throw may be augmented by placing your right elbow under Uke's left armpit.

Breaking Uke's balance forwards, step in as for *kubi nage*. Bend your knees so that your hips are in contact with the front of Uke's thighs. Gripping the back of Uke's collar, thrust your right elbow under Uke's left armpit (or thrust your right arm straight up if this is possible) and use it to lift Uke strongly as you straighten your knees. Thrust your hips back and turn to throw Uke over your hip.

Remember to let go with your right hand as Uke falls to enable Uke to breakfall, and maintain control of the technique with your left hand on Uke's right sleeve. This particular technique was only introduced into the Zen Family syllabus during 1987, and extends the standing techniques to a total of 42. Prior to this only *sode tsuri komi goshi* was taught.

SODE TSURI KOMI GOSHI

This version of the technique is simpler to perform and is quite effective against an opponent who maintains stiff arms. It is even more important to remember to let go of Uke's sleeve as you perform the technique.

Catching Uke's left sleeve from the outside with your right hand, lift the sleeve up into the air and turn in as for *kubi nage*. Whilst thrusting Uke's sleeve upwards and forwards bend your knees and pull Uke's right arm in to your chest. Straighten your knees and thrust your hips backwards whilst turning and throwing.

To help one remember this throw, as it has a name which is easily confused with others, it is termed the 'windmill', perhaps because your upstretched arm moves round in a windmill fashion as you throw. To understand the thinking behind this throw you need to refer to a text on *nage-no-kata* to see how it is performed. There it is used as the augmenting of a normal hip throw after Uke resists backwards.

UCHI ASHI GAKE

This is a variation of the basic trip throw, *ashi gake*, and you now see this technique being performed on the other leg by moving inside (*uchi*). This leads the student towards the major inner reaping throw, *o uchi gari*, at a later stage.

Turn the right side of your body in to Uke's body, sliding your right hand under the left armpit to lift-pull Uke towards your left side. Pass your right leg between Uke's legs and around the left leg to put your toes on the mat outside Uke's left foot. Pull up and around to your right with both hands, pushing Uke back to your front right-hand corner.

This technique is based on the presumption that Uke will begin to resist as you begin to break his or her balance by your pull to your left side. Your turn and throw to the opposite corner should coincide with Uke's resistance in that direction. One common fault is that Tori will fail to complete the throw with a turning movement to the right. Uke must land almost at right angles to Tori due to the turn in the finish of this throw.

Uchi ashi gake

KO SOTO GARI

This technique cannot be executed from standing and so, like most of the other foot sweeps, is taught on the move. There appears to be some controversy over the naming of the foot sweeps, and you may well encounter this technique described as *de ashi bari* (or *harai*) in other manuals. This depends upon the original Japanese Sensei who taught the style, as many have tended to differ over some throws. The techniques themselves are quite dissimilar, although the illustrations or photographs tend to look very much the same.

As you walk in step with Uke, forwards or backwards, take a quick step with your right foot, placing your weight firmly on to that foot. Using the side of your left foot quickly sweep

Ko soto gari

it across the front of your body, taking Uke's right ankle as it advances (or retreats), and sweeping it to your right side. At the same time pull downwards with your left hand on Uke's sleeve to complete the throw.

Another method of executing the same technique may be by pushing Uke backwards and upwards to the right rear corner, taking your right leg and placing it to your rear just outside Uke's bodyline. As you do this place the sole of your left foot at the side of Uke's right heel and sweep this leg slightly forward and across Uke's body.

There is little doubt that this technique can be difficult for beginners to the grade, and much practice is required walking up and down the mat to sweep at every opportunity. The throw must be practised forwards and backwards.

HIKI TAI

This is probably the most easily remembered technique in the syllabus and is a smooth and powerful throw when executed correctly. The throw requires a downward spiral movement on the part of Tori to demonstrate the technique to its best effect.

Move in as for *kubi nage*, gripping Uke's right sleeve with both hands, one above the other, and tucking your right elbow under Uke's right arm. Pull Uke's right sleeve across your chest, turning your hip in and around. As you continue your downward spiral turn, Uke is thrown by the leverage.

The key to this throw is where you grip Uke's sleeve. Too high up the arm and you will have difficulty tucking your elbow in. Too low and you will separate from Uke, losing much of the impetus. The grip should be midway down the sleeve.

UCHI ASHI SASAE

This technique utilises two changes in Uke's direction of resistance. As you step back Uke will begin to resist to the rear. When you subsequently block to the rear of Uke's foot, the resistance changes to a forwards direction to counter the expected throw to the rear. Your completion of the techique to Uke's front thus blends with the resistance. There are two ways to execute this throw:

(a) Step backwards slightly with your left foot, pulling Uke strongly forwards to make a step with the right foot. Slide your right foot behind Uke's right foot and turn to your left pulling with your left hand on Uke's sleeve. Uke's momentum will help you to complete the throw.

(b) Turn the right side of your body in to Uke's body. As you do, pass your right leg between Uke's legs and block the rear of Uke's right foot. Pull up and around with your left hand whilst at the same time pushing up and around in a circular motion with your right hand. The throw is circular, to Uke's front right-hand corner.

KATA ASHI DORI

This technique, like *ryo ashi dori* earlier, relies upon surprise for its execution. The positioning of Tori's hand during the throw is important only in that it must be at around Uke's knee level. You may place the hand to the rear of Uke's knee from outside or inside, or you may grasp the *gi* at knee level to complete the throw. The technique is described with only one hand position, but bear in mind that there are alternatives.

Place your right foot outside Uke's right foot, at the same time pulling Uke's right sleeve to his or her rear right-hand corner. As you do this, place your right hand behind Uke's right thigh, at about knee level, to prevent Uke from stepping back. With your left leg take a long step forward, passing Uke's body over and curving yourself to the left as you throw.

A common fault with this technique is that Tori will tend to block Uke's right ankle with the right foot as in *ashi gake*. This should not be done, the block being supplied by the hand alone.

BLUE TO BROWN BELT

It is expected that the student will take about one year between blue and brown belt gradings. Much of this time will be taken up with teaching lower belts, and the blue belt is expected to assume a degree of responsibility within the club. As you attain higher grades, so the amount of formal instruction that you receive becomes correspondingly less. The accent in training with higher grades is on *randori*, as it is more important than ever now to be able to utilise the techniques that you have been taught.

The techniques within this syllabus are not particularly difficult providing you have mastered the previous gradings. What is difficult is the grading that you will have to go through next. The brown belt grading is probably the most difficult, in physical terms, that you will meet. A high standard of knowledge is expected and an exceptional degree of stamina is required to complete the grading, as I found to my cost the first time that I took it.

It must be pointed out that groundholds are now to be performed to both right and left sides. This is a fairly recent requirement and instructors should take care to pay special attention to this when teaching the groundholds syllabus.

SOTO GAKE

This technique follows roughly the lines of *ko soto gake* in the orange to green belt syllabus, only performed with more power. The pushing action of hands and arms is combined with an outside hook of the foot to make this a potentially heavy throw to the rear.

Soto gake

Soto gake – Note that Tori's left heel is in contact with the rear of Uke's right knee. In this case Tori's right hand is grasping Uke's gi and pulling strongly downwards.

Move your right foot forward to a point midway between Uke's legs. With your left hand push downwards towards Uke's right heel. Slide your right hand over Uke's shoulder and push down to the rear, effectively pinning Uke on his or her heels. Hook your left foot behind Uke's right knee from the outside, pulling it forwards to complete the throw.

One common fault is that students will tend to grip under Uke's left shoulder, as in *ko soto gake*. So long as they hold the *gi* and pull down, this is permissible; otherwise they should carry the right arm over the shoulder.

HARAI TSURI KOMI ASHI

This is one of the more difficult techniques in the syllabus and relies upon timing and balance. It is all the more difficult if your partner is heavier than you. It may be taught as a walking technique as in *ko soto gari*, or as a one-step technique as shown here.

As Uke steps forward with the left leg, slide your right foot forward to a point inside his or her left foot, but in front of Uke's right foot. At the same time, with the sole of your left foot sweep Uke's right ankle back behind his or her left leg, pulling out and round with your left hand whilst lifting up and round with your right hand.

Students may find it easier to perform the lift with both hands at first until the timing of the throw becomes familiar. You should not use this throw as an excuse to hack at Uke's ankles during *randori*; it spoils the look of your Judo if you are hacking all the time. Many contest players adopt this habit as a method of disguising their real intent, and while this may be quite acceptable within a competition, it is not acceptable in *randori* on a Zen Family mat where most players are there to enjoy themselves.

Harai tsuri komi ashi

O SOTO GARI

This is one of the potentially more dangerous throws in the syllabus. Essentially it is a simple technique which can be particularly hard on Uke when performed swiftly and without notice. When practising, it is advisable for the instructor to tell Uke to put his or her weight on the other leg so that the sweep will not have too devastating an effect.

Step in as for *ashi gake*, swinging your right leg through the gap between your left leg and Uke's legs. Circle it round the back of Uke's right leg keeping the toe pointing downwards. Sweep your leg backwards, driving your head and shoulders forwards and downwards. The point of contact is between the back of your right thigh and the back of Uke's right thigh.

One common fault is when Tori swings his or her leg through and too far forward before driving it back to perform the technique. The second or so that this delays the throw is sufficient to alert Uke to what is happening and provide time

O soto gari – This sweep utilises the whole body, not just Tori's leg. Note Tori's posture as Uke's leg is swept from under him.

to counter. The leg should be hooked in and the throw completed from this position.

SUMI OTOSHI

This is a corner circular throw which is not seen very much these days. Its usefulness will by now have become apparent, however, as it is the movement of the standard counter practised from white belt onwards. Now it comes of age as a throw in its own right.

With your hands lift Uke up and to the front right corner of his or her body. As you do this, turn your left leg and step away from Uke, pointing the foot in the direction in which Uke is facing. Turn your right foot in the same direction and rise up on your toes. With your hands continue the circular movement to your left front corner to complete the throw.

The step back should carry your weight back so as to unbalance Uke forwards, and this momentum is continued into the throw. Try to retain control of Uke after the throw by keeping hold of the sleeve. There is a tendency for Uke to roll away after this throw if you do not hold tightly.

HIJI OTOSHI

This technique is essentially the same as *sumi otoshi*, except that the hands grip the sleeves just above the elbows.

Grip Uke's right sleeve just above the elbow with your left hand, thumb pointing towards Uke. With your right hand take hold of Uke's left sleeve just above the elbow with your thumb pointing away from Uke. Lift upwards and to the right front corner of Uke's body. Turn your left leg and make one long step away and round to Uke's left front corner. Pull Uke on and off the side of your hip, continuing the circular movement to your left front corner.

The comments on this techique are exactly the same as for *sumi otoshi*.

HANE GOSHI

A difficult technique to perform correctly without much practice, as it involves utilising your balance as you lift Uke on your hip. The translation 'spring hip' indicates that it is a very active throw in which Tori must do a lot of work. The stance is important, so read the description carefully. Note that you do not go in as far as you would for *kubi nage*: your left foot slides to only half-way round.

Hane goshi

Hane goshi – Uke must be held close as Tori springs his hip and leg upwards. Note Uke's weight is all but taken on to Tori's right leg and hip.

Break Uke's balance to the front with a lift-pull on the right sleeve and a pull with your right hand. Step in with your right foot to a point midway between Uke's legs. Turn and point your left foot away from Uke, toes pointing in the direction that Uke is facing. Raise your right leg, bend it at the knee and place it across the front of Uke's legs with your knee projecting beyond Uke's right knee. At the same time pass your right arm around Uke's neck (or back if Uke is taller than you). Now with both hands hold Uke's body tightly to your side and sway your weight to your left, lifting Uke clear of the mat, over your hip and down.

With children, one of the problems is that they cannot always lift Uke in this throw because their muscle development is not sufficient. In such cases it is enough for them to show the movement for grading purposes. Uke will naturally land at your side, as in *koshi guruma*, if you complete the throw correctly.

KATA GURUMA

This is not a technique which one will perform readily, even during *randori*. It relies upon Uke attacking Tori in a certain manner and is usually a slow technique compared to most others. It is easily countered and blocked by Uke.

Kata guruma

Kata guruma – Tori must balance Uke carefully to lift him in this fashion. In this case the throw will be executed forwards over Tori's head.

Pull on Uke's right sleeve with your left hand so that Uke advances the right foot. Step in with your right foot between Uke's legs, bending your knees to lower your body. Put your right hand between Uke's legs, taking hold of his or her right thigh with your shoulder in the groin. With your right hand lift Uke on to your shoulders and throw Uke over your head so that he or she falls obliquely to your left front corner.

It is important to remember to bend your knees and not lean forward when practising this technique. You can severely strain your back when attempting a bad lift. Always ensure that Uke's belt is placed over your neck so that the weight is distributed evenly across your shoulders.

The grading to 1st Kyu, apart from being physically exhausting, places emphasis upon knowledge of basic technique. The throws which are taught at earlier stages must be faultless and any lack of knowledge in these areas is an early indication of failure. Leeway may be given in some areas providing the student demonstrates a good understanding of the requirements. Most of the techniques are required to be performed to the left as well as to the right and it is accepted that you will probably be a bit shaky with left-hand throws, counters, and so on. Left-hand groundholds can prove to be somewhat tricky at first, but these are easily mastered with practice.

The point of this grading is that when the student is invited to try for black belt, he or she will have been through all the main techniques that can be requested. This is the final grading that is completed at the standard grading sessions. The next grading will be at the discretion of the Master of Zen Judo after consultation with your chief instructor.

BROWN TO BLACK BELT

The time taken between brown and black belt will be at least one year, during which time the player will be mainly teaching lower grades. Instruction in the final techniques required for 1st Dan will be limited to a few special sessions under the senior instructor. 1st Kyu grades are expected to be able to retain most of what they have learned, and the majority of their practising is during *randori*.

So, at last you have gained your brown belt after much hard work; what is your status within the club? Well, several things will change for you at this time. Firstly, you are now expected to stand on the other side of the mat with the instructors at all sessions, and with this goes certain responsibilities. You must help to keep order or discipline on the mat. You may be asked to check the general cleanliness (hands, nails, feet) of juniors coming on to the mat. You are expected to help organise the juniors as they walk around the mat so that they line up correctly; and you must give help where necessary in classes, for example in demonstrating how to tie belts and how to perform exercises and in spotting wristwatches and jewellery which may have been forgotten as players come on to the mat.

Secondly, it is now your task to conduct gradings for white to yellow and yellow to orange belts. You will be guided in the beginning by a Dan grade so that you understand the process and what to look for. Whilst performing gradings is relatively easy, and may be considered boring, you must remember that the players being graded are expecting as much from you in the form of involvement as they are putting into their grading. This is enlarged upon in the chapter on gradings.

Finally, as prospective black belts it is up to you to set an example for the rest of the students to follow, both in your general conduct and in your performance of Judo. Whilst you are busy setting these examples for the lower grades to follow, you yourself are being gradually assessed by your chief instructor. He or she is watching for your willingness to help lower grades, your patience with juniors who need extra guidance, your self-discipline during *randori*, and the way in which you keep order when this is necessary. All these qualities, and others, contribute towards the final recommendation for grading to 1st Dan.

In Zen Judo the original Japanese system of grading assessment still operates. If the candidate appears to be the wrong type, for one reason or another, but has managed to attain 1st Kyu (which is most unlikely), he or she may never be called up for a black belt grading. Having said that, there are several who will manage or have managed to get through this net because of personality changes after gaining their Dan grades. Even with the most sophisticated system this will happen, and there is little that can be done about it.

The techniques taught in this section are more or less the basic fighting techniques used by other forms of Judo. By this time you should be well co-ordinated and controlled, and capable of using the following techniques without endangering your Uke. The full syllabus is given in appendix A.

Okuri ashi barai

OKURI ASHI BARAI

This throw is generally performed at the end of a series of side skips. Such a movement is rarely met with in reality and thus the throw will appear artificial. The description given below is for this throw to be performed in a more real-life manner.

Get Uke to step forward with the left foot by pulling with your right hand. As Uke puts weight on this foot you pull forwards and upwards with your hands to Uke's front left corner. At the same time step back with your right leg to your left rear. Now get Uke to take another step forward with the right foot and place the sole of your left foot on the outside of Uke's right foot as it comes into line with the left foot. Push Uke's right foot into the left foot, moving Uke's weight with your hands from the front left corner to the front right corner. Sweep Uke's feet up to complete the throw.

O UCHI GARI

This technique is similar to *uchi ashi gake* in the green to blue syllabus, but it tends to be more basic whilst having a harder effect upon Uke.

Pushing with your hands, drive Uke back and upwards to the left rear corner. Whilst doing this, turn the right side of your body into Uke's body. Pass your right leg between Uke's legs and around his or her left leg in a circular motion, the calf of your right leg making contact with the lower part of Uke's left leg. Straighten your left leg and sweep back with your right whilst continuing to push forward and to Uke's left rear corner.

O uchi gari

50

The commonest fault that Tori commits is that of losing his or her balance and falling over Uke when the throw is complete. The forward thrust must only be sufficient to compensate Uke's resistance.

UCHI MATA

This being one of the main techniques of Judo, it warrants a longer description than has been given for many others. There are many ways to perform the technique but I will deal only with three in this text. A well-executed *uchi mata* can be an extremely heavy throw, which is most useful in a defensive situation and will give you a quick advantage over your aggressor.

(a) Grip Uke's sleeve and the back of the collar. Slide your left foot across so that it is almost in front of your right foot. Pivot on the ball of the left foot bringing your right leg through between yourself and Uke as you turn. Pull Uke up and on to you, swinging your right leg up and between Uke's legs. Your right thigh should sweep Uke's inner right thigh upwards to complete the throw.

(b) Pulling gently on Uke's left lapel, make him or her advance the left foot. As Uke does so step in with your left foot to a point midway between Uke's legs. As Uke is about to transfer weight from the right foot to the left, insert your right leg between Uke's legs, turning in and sweeping Uke's left leg upwards with your inner right thigh from inside.

(c) Step back and around with your left foot to a point just outside Uke's left foot, turning your body as you do this. Break Uke's balance forwards with a pull by both hands so that Uke's balance is on the toes. Insert your right leg between Uke's legs, continuing to turn to the left. Lift your right leg under Uke's left thigh, pulling forwards and downwards with your left hand, turning Uke off your raised right leg to complete the throw.

Uchi mata – Uke's balance has been broken forwards prior to applying this technique. Note that Tori's arm is well around Uke's neck whilst his action is similar to that in *o soto gari*.

DE ASHI BARAI

Aside from some confusion between this technique and *ko soto gari*, this particular technique can be very difficult to comprehend for some. I have seen players who could never get the rhythm of the move however much they tried. Here I describe two separate methods of accomplishing the technique.

De ashi barai

(a) Step back with your right leg, placing your foot to the rear of your left foot. Pull on Uke's sleeve to encourage a step forward with the right foot. Keeping your weight on your right foot, as Uke is about to put the foot on to the mat, place the sole of your left foot behind Uke's advancing foot and sweep this leg forwards and towards Uke's front left corner. With your hands turn Uke's body to the front right-hand corner.

(b) Take a normal step back with your left foot, Uke following in step. Step back and round with your right foot so that it is placed on the mat behind your left foot. Uke takes another normal step forwards, with the left foot. Swing your weight on to your right foot so that Uke will begin to take a further step with the right leg. At this point place the sole of your left foot behind Uke's advancing foot and continue the movement forwards in the direction of Uke's advance with a sweeping action. Thus Uke loses control of the step as if the leg has slipped forwards. This technique is often nicknamed the 'banana skin' throw for this reason.

The important part of this technique is the second step, where you effectively take your body out of Uke's line of approach, allowing Uke to pass in front of you as you blend with the forward movement to effect the sweep.

HARAI GOSHI

This is another fairly simple sweeping hip technique only utilising the basic movements. The fact that Uke's legs are swept upwards, and the subsequent fall, can be somewhat frightening to the beginner and so puts the throw into this final syllabus. Two slightly differing descriptions are given, but there are several more ways to effect this technique.

(a) Slide your right hand under Uke's left arm, bringing it up so that your arm is bent and pulling Uke on to you. Take a small step back with your left foot, turning your back to Uke. Bring your right leg outside Uke's right leg and sweep it up to Uke's loin, throwing Uke over your right hip and leg by this action.

(b) Break Uke's balance forwards by a lift-pull with both hands. Enter as in *kubi nage* so that your feet are inside Uke's feet, slipping your right arm around Uke's back. Sway your weight on to your left foot so you can raise your right foot off the ground. Turn to your left and sweep your right leg backwards and up, taking Uke's legs off the ground with the back of your right thigh to throw Uke down in front of you.

This is similar to *uchi mata* except that you are sweeping both of Uke's legs at the same time. Close control is essential, and failure to pull Uke on to you as you enter is the commonest fault.

KO UCHI GARI

This appears to be a simple little technique, but it needs precise timing to perfect. It makes a useful second technique as a follow-up to *o uchi gari* if this fails to work, as long as your change of direction is swift. Two descriptions are given here: the first is that mainly used by the popular forms of European Judo, whilst the second is the technique originally taught by Sensei McCarthy and expected during gradings.

Ko uchi gari – This version of the technique is pulling Uke's right leg around and away from him. Tori has now only to push lightly to complete the technique

(a) Pushing with your hands, drive Uke back and upward to the left rear corner. Whilst doing this, turn the right side of your body into Uke's body. Pass your right leg between Uke's legs and place the inside of your right foot to the back of Uke's right heel, sweeping this leg towards Uke's front.

(b) Step back with your left foot and place it behind and in line with your right foot, toes pointing to Uke's right front corner. Turn your body as you do this, so that your left shoulder is moving away and the resulting pull on Uke's right sleeve will make Uke step forward on the right foot. As Uke does this, with the sole of your right foot sweep Uke's right foot forwards and round to your left in a circular motion. Pull forwards with your left hand on Uke's right sleeve and push up and back with your right hand to Uke's right rear to complete the throw.

Having practised the two methods, you will notice how different they are. The second method requires careful timing and is a delicate and satisfying technique to accomplish, much more in keeping with the spirit of Zen Judo.

O GOSHI

This final technique is probably the first to be taught in European-style Judo, and provides for good control throughout the throw. This throw is, however, capable of being 'laid on' very heavily, and any lack of control may render it a first-class deterrent. Two methods are described: the first is taught only in Zen clubs whilst the second is the more universal technique. Both methods will be required during your grading.

O goshi

(a) Turn in so that your feet are inside Uke's feet with your left foot to the rear of your right. Turn your body, bending the knees to deepen your hip towards Uke's right side, and set the left side of your back into Uke's body. Slide your right hand over Uke's shoulder and around the neck to the right shoulder. Pull Uke's right arm across your chest by the sleeve, curving your body forward and downward until your right knee makes contact with the mat, giving impetus to the throw.

(b) Lift and pull Uke slightly with both hands, stepping in with your right foot to just inside Uke's right foot. Slide your right arm under Uke's left armpit and around the shoulder as you turn in with your left foot inside Uke's left foot. Keeping your knees bent, project your right hip and pick Uke up on to it as you straighten your knees. Complete the throw by turning and bringing Uke over your hip to land in front of you.

You will notice the amount of control that you have over Uke at all times during this technique. The first method requires more hip movement, and ideally Uke should land

180 degrees from the original position, that is, Uke is carried straight over your back with legs straight out from you. Note also that you finish in the ideal position to slide into a groundhold. Your right arm should be cushioning Uke's head at the moment of breakfall.

IN CONCLUSION

This completes the syllabus of 42 throws with which you are required to be thoroughly familiar. More throws will be given at a later stage in your studies, but these constitute the main Zen repertoire. Many players who come to Zen from other styles fail to understand the rationale behind this syllabus, because the throws they see as basic have mainly been left to the end.

If you study the syllabus carefully in the manner in which it is laid out, you can see that the initial throws are only basic moves which get the student entering and turning correctly. These are followed by simple throws which do not deter the nervous student from practice, as the feet remain on the ground. Once orange grade has been attained, study proceeds in earnest and the high throws commence. The feet will leave the mat in increasing height, and the student is put through a set of techniques requiring precision in balance.

From this point the syllabus gives several 'precursor' techniques such as *uchi ashi gake*, *o soto otoshi* and *uchi ashi sasae* to train the student to be ready for techniques coming later. At blue belt stage we see the introduction of the first 'strength' techniques such as *kata guruma*, *sumi otoshi*, and so on, which tend to rely on Tori's power to complete or enter into the throw. Finally the last seven techniques are, in the main, the harder competitive throws which can be applied with as much force as you wish.

The foot sweeps, which again require precision of balance, are introduced at green belt stage and upwards as these can be quite painful when badly applied.

Sacrifice techniques, preceded by half-sacrifices, are carefully controlled on the mat, being only gently introduced at green belt stage after the player has many months of practice.

There is little doubt that this syllabus, compiled in this fashion, is designed to cater for the student who wishes to perform the techniques of Judo in a highly controlled and technical manner. For those who want to go on to the mat and hammer one another around the canvas, there are other styles catering for this desire. Zen students are trained slowly and with extreme care; the end result of the training given in this book being a black belt who has a wealth of technique and teaching experience to draw upon, and who understands how to care for lower-grade students.

4
COMBINATION TECHNIQUES

A major part of the Zen syllabus takes the form of combination techniques for all grades. Even the initial grading requires the student to present a basic understanding of movement from one throw to another. Each successive grading requires a further extension of the combinations in use, either in number or in complexity.

When you are practising on the move, and the desired throw is not successful – either because it has been entered in error or because Uke has not been unbalanced – it is essential to be able to swiftly adapt the throw to another complimentary technique. Often a completely opposite technique will meet with success if Uke over-compensates at your first or second attempt.

Combinations can thus be divided into two basic movements, those of *balance reversal*, where you alter the throw to take Uke the opposite way to your first movement, and *additive techniques*, where each additional technique breaks Uke's balance a little more until the final throwing technique is applied.

BALANCE REVERSAL

Some examples of this type of technique would be the following combinations:

Kubi nage technique two – Tori enters for *kubi nage* but has not broken Uke's balance properly.

Tori begins to change direction and technique.

Tori is now in position to throw Uke backwards with *ko uchi maki komi.*

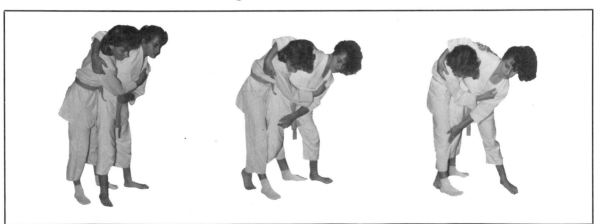

Kubi Nage/Ko Uchi Maki Komi

This combination would work with hip or hand throws like *tai otoshi*, *kata seoi*, *eri nage* or *hiki tai*. Several of these techniques can be strung together to finish with *ko uchi maki komi*.

Kata Seoi/Ashi Gake or O Soto Otoshi

This outside combination can be developed to combine one or more hand throws with a suitable rear throw.

Kata seoi technique two – Tori enters for *kata seoi* sufficiently for Uke to begin to pull back.

As Uke pulls back, Tori changes direction by turning to the right.

Tori can now throw with *ashi gake*.

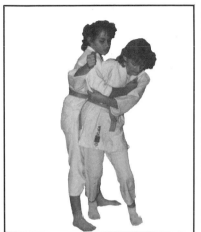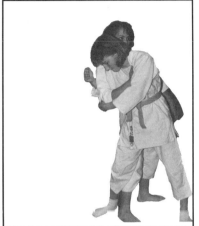

Ko Uchi Gari/O Uchi Gari

This is a simple reversal of balance where Tori blends with Uke's resistance to the minor foot sweep.

Ashi Gake/Tai Otoshi

This again shows a rear throw turned to complete a successful hand throw in a forward direction.

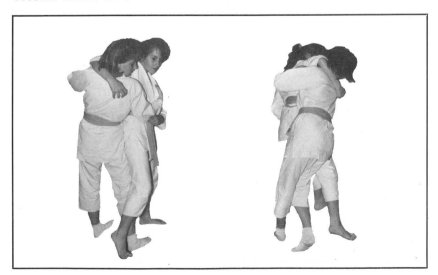

Ashi gake technique two – Having entered for *ashi gake*, Tori swivels to the rear on the right foot.

Tori can now throw Uke with *tai otoshi*.

ADDITIVE TECHNIQUES

The following techniques would be examples of additive combinations:

Kubi Nage/Tai Otoshi/Koshi Guruma

This combination simply relies upon movement of the right foot more deeply at each stage until the final throw.

Kubi nage technique three – Tori enters for *kubi nage* but fails to fully break Uke's balance forwards.

Tori extends the right foot into *tai otoshi*. Note that the left foot remains in its original position.

Tori's posture is further extended into *koshi guruma*, breaking Uke's balance further forwards to enable the technique to be completed.

Te Hiza Sasae/Kata Seoi/Tai Otoshi

This combination shows firstly a single movement of the right hand, followed by a step across Uke's right leg. You do not move your hand from the *kata seoi* position.

Sode Tsuri Komi Goshi/Kata Nage/Uki Goshi/Obi Goshi

This technique four shows another simple hand movement. The first throw involves your right arm pushing upwards upon Uke's sleeve. You let go of the sleeve, allowing Uke's arm to fall over your elbow into *kata nage*. You place your hand around the waist for *uki goshi*, then grip the belt to throw in *obi goshi*.

Ko Soto Gake/Ashi Gake/O Soto Otoshi/O Soto Guruma

In this technique four you step from the first to the second throw simply by bringing your left foot to the side and following through with your right foot into *ashi gake*. The stamp is not completed if you wish to pass to the final throw as you break Uke's balance fully.

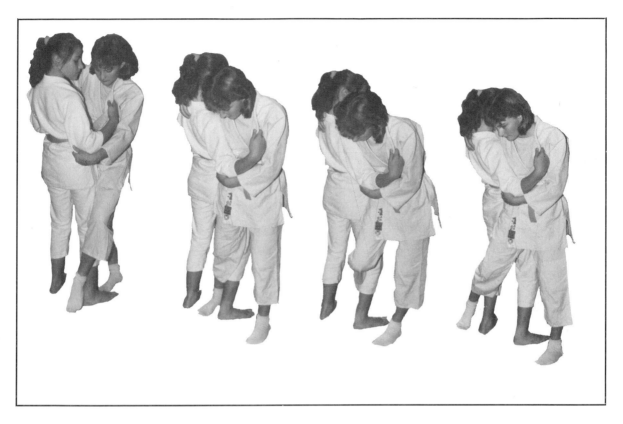

TECHNIQUE TWOS—FIVES

The terminology used for combination throws is 'technique two, three, four or five', referring to the number of separate throws which must be combined in each demonstration. Thus a technique two is a combination of two throws, one following from the other, the second throw being effective. A technique four would combine four techniques, throwing on the fourth technique. It is quite possible to combine many more techniques, and the execution of technique sevens, tens and so on, are not uncommon in certain teaching situations.

Two useful objectives of these combinations are ease of revision, and to show your instructor that you are completely familiar with your syllabus of throws.

The essence of successful combination techniques in Zen Judo is firstly to progress from throw to throw with the minimum of movement. Only one foot or hand movement is expected. The removal of your arm from behind the neck or back of Uke to a frontal position, such as *uki goshi* to *kata seoi*, is not an acceptable progression, neither is undue hand and foot movement at the same time. Secondly, the combination should be capable of use in *randori* as a variable technique, even though it is unlikely that anything beyond a technique two or three could be justifiably utilised.

Ko soto gake technique four — Tori steps forward into *ko soto gake* without breaking Uke's balance too far.

Tori now steps around Uke into *ashi gake*, breaking Uke's balance further to the rear.

Tori raises her leg to perform *o soto otoshi*, but does not complete the stamp.

Tori follows through to completely break Uke's balance by applying *o soto guruma*.

When improvising with these combinations, it is advisable to ensure that your final throw is a simple one requiring little in the way of balance or special footwork. For instance, to finish a technique three or four with such throws as *o guruma*, *ashi guruma*, *hane goshi* or *eri nage* is asking a great deal, as these techniques depend upon perfect balance, precise footwork or exact hand placing. If they are to be incorporated within the combination, try to ensure that they come towards the beginning.

Special care should be taken when using *o soto guruma* within a combination as this technique tends to commit your balance completely to Uke's rear right corner, and it may be impossible to recover from this move when you are in the middle of a complicated combination.

Students are advised to keep in mind several set combinations which fall naturally together – or happen to suit you – as during grading sessions a combination technique will be required to every throw in your syllabus. Certain throws are practised only occasionally and these often do not lend themselves to incorporation within combination techniques. Such throws are *ryo ashi dori*, *ko soto gari*, *eri nage*, *kata ashi dori*, *uchi ashi sasae*, *sumi otoshi* and *hiji otoshi*. The following lists are examples of acceptable combinations for these throws.

Ryo Ashi Dori/Kata Seoi

Rising up from *ryo ashi dori*, grasp Uke's right sleeve and turn in to bring your right arm up under Uke's right armpit. Further combinations will follow from this position if needed.

Ko Soto Gari/Uchi Ashi Sasae/Uchi Ashi Gake

As you begin to sweep with your left foot, stop the technique about a third of the way across, allowing Uke to put his or her foot on to the mat. Step forward with your right foot to the inside of Uke's right foot, blocking to the rear of it. Bring your weight on to your left foot as you turn to your left. From this combination pull Uke towards you with your right hand, hooking your right leg back around Uke's left calf, toes on the mat. Further combinations can follow from this position.

Eri Nage/Seoi Nage/Te Hiza Sasae

Turn in to *eri nage*. Having paused a moment, let go with your left hand and grasp Uke's right sleeve, pulling it across your chest. Let your elbow rise under Uke's right armpit. After a further pause, let go with your right hand, bringing your arm down so that the right hand is over Uke's knee in *te hiza sasae*. Other throws are now open to follow from this combination.

Kata Ashi Dori/Kata Seoi

Walk into *kata ashi dori*, right foot and right hand leading. From the 'in' position reverse your balance, taking your left foot back and round and bringing your right arm up under Uke's right armpit into *kata seoi*.

Sumi Otoshi/Ashi Guruma/Tai Otoshi

This will also work for *hiji otoshi*, and a similar combination may be utilised. As you turn to your left, do not exert force to pull Uke round but stop momentarily to indicate *sumi (hiji) otoshi*. After this pause, carry your left foot round until it is pointing in the same direction as Uke's, with your back to him or her. Slide your arm around Uke's neck and extend your right foot into *ashi guruma*. Lower your right foot to the mat outside Uke's right foot into *tai otoshi*.

With *hiji otoshi*, a similar movement could produce *o guruma* if you slide your hand under Uke's armpit and round the back, raising your right leg higher. From this position your best move would be to carry the combination into *uki goshi*, *obi goshi*, *kata nage* and finish with *tai otoshi* if a technique five is required.

Other combination techniques are used within the Zen syllabus, such as half-sacrifice and full sacrifice twos and threes; however these will be discussed under the general heading of sacrifice techniques. As you will notice from the foregoing, the concept of combination techniques can become quite complicated and will require an in-depth knowledge of the total syllabus available to the student being graded. This is one method of ensuring that the Zen student becomes thoroughly familiar with each syllabus before proceeding to a higher grade. This, of course, is only one of the forms used in grading – several others will be practised as well.

In conclusion, the practice of these movements, apart from increasing your knowledge of the syllabus, will help to improve your sense of balance and give you a 'feel' for your partner's balance and movement. One good way to practise technique threes and fours is to do it blindfold, relying only on your sense of touch and balance to tell you how your partner is positioned. In *randori* the Dan grades will often be seen performing with their eyes shut or fixed on a spot over Uke's shoulder or head, using only feel to guide them.

5
COUNTERS TO STANDING TECHNIQUES

A major section of the Zen syllabus concerns the techniques for countering all the various throws. The counters used are of several varieties, being taught under the nomenclature of 'counter ones', 'counter twos' and counter 'two-by-twos'. There are also sacrifice counters, but these will be discussed in the chapter on sacrifice techniques.

The initial grading to yellow belt is concerned only with the student becoming familiar with a simple counter technique, the basis of the throw *sumi otoshi*, which features in its own right within the blue to brown syllabus. The subsequent grading to orange belt necessitates the student being familiar with both counter ones and twos.

Further gradings require the student to become accomplished at counter two-by-twos and, later, sacrifice counters. Counter throws, although not often required, should be practised to both right- and left-hand throws to ensure that the student is thoroughly familiar with their application.

COUNTER ONES

As Uke turns in to throw you in a hand or hip throw, you step back with your left foot, pivoting on the ball of your right foot, and transfer your weight to your rear with your

Counter one – Uke enters for a throw and, as he does so, Tori begins to turn to her left and step back.

Tori's step-back complete, she transfers her weight to her left foot, drawing Uke past her to throw in the counter.

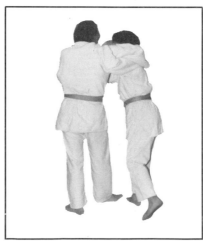 

backward step. This has the effect of blending your movement with the forward thrust of Uke as he or she enters for the throw, carrying Uke past you to breakfall on the mat to your left. The further you step back, the further your weight will move from its original position, and thus the more impetus will be imparted to Uke. If Uke is moving in a strong forward direction, he or she will be carried well past you. Here Julia is shown countering Ken's *kubi nage* attempt. Note the strong step back with her left foot taken as Ken is turning in for his throw.

This basic counter can be used successfully on the majority of throws in the syllabus. There are, however, a few notable exceptions which are listed as follows:

Hiza Guruma

The counter to *hiza guruma* can be performed with a different blending of movement from that described above, namely blending with the turning movement of this throw.

As Uke moves round, raising the left foot towards your right knee to perform *hiza guruma*, you blend with this movement by stepping over this foot with your right leg so that the rising foot comes between your legs. As you are turning to your left, continue the motion and raise your left foot to Uke's right knee before Uke's left foot can be completely lowered to the mat. Utilising the normal technique with your hands, you can now throw Uke in right *hiza guruma*.

Ryo Ashi Dori

As Uke squats down in front of you, keep hold of the left lapel but let go with your left hand. Place your left hand on the back of Uke's belt, grasping it lightly. Step back with your

Counter one to ryo ashi dori – As Uke enters for *ryo ashi dori*, Tori steps back, turning to the left and grasping Uke's belt at the back.

The step-back complete, Tori turns and throws Uke in the counter.

left foot, pulling up and around with your left hand to turn Uke over with a lift of your right hand. Here Ken executes this counter to Laurence's throw.

Sasae Tsuri Komi Ashi

This counter follows a similar pattern to *hiza guruma*. As Uke tries to break your balance forwards, step quickly over the propping foot with your right leg towards your right front corner. Push Uke backwards with your right hand on the lapel so that Uke resists forwards. As Uke does this, bring your left foot up to the side of Uke's right knee and throw in right *hiza guruma*.

Ko Soto Gari

As Uke tries to sweep your right foot across your body with his or her left foot, step over the sweeping foot to counter-sweep Uke's left foot in *ko soto gari*, utilising the original sweeping momentum to unbalance Uke and complete the throw. Julia's step-over here occurs early in the sweep, giving her time to sweep Ken's foot into left *ko soto gari*.

Counter one to ko soto gari – Uke begins to sweep Tori's foot in *ko soto gari* and Tori prepares to step over Uke's sweeping foot.

Tori now begins to sweep with her right foot.

Tori's counter is complete as Uke's foot is swept away.

Harai Tsuri Komi Ashi

You take a half-step forward with your left foot as Uke enters with a half-step with the right foot. Uke will lift-pull you to the front and sweep with the left foot. As Uke's pull is felt, transfer your weight to your left foot, extend your right leg forwards between Uke's legs and around Uke's left calf in *o uchi gari* or *uchi ashi gake*, depending on your grade.

Uchi Ashi Gake/O Uchi Gari

The counter to these throws is essentially the same. As Uke slides his or her right leg between your legs to execute the throw, transfer your weight to your left foot. Lean forwards, passing your right leg between Uke's legs and around the left calf and into *uchi ashi gake* or *o uchi gari* depending on your grade.

De Ashi Barai

As Uke begins to sweep your right foot, allow it to be carried only a short distance, turning to your left and bringing your back towards Uke. Place your right foot on the mat just outside Uke's right foot, and continue your turn to throw Uke in *tai otoshi*.

Counter one to harai tsuri komi ashi – Uke is stepping in to perform harai tsuri komi ashi.

Tori eases forward before Uke can perform his sweep.

Tori slides his foot in and counters with o ochi gari.

Counter one to de ashi bari – Uke commences to sweep Tori's right foot in de ashi bari.

Tori puts his foot on the mat and turns in for a counter throw.

The counter (seoi nage) is applied to good effect.

Okuri Ashi Barai

This throw is demonstrated for standing technique in the same form as in *nage no kata*, utilising three side steps and throwing on the third step. Your counter is to take a longer skip on the second step, dropping your hand to Uke's belt and lifting as Uke completes the second skip, to throw Uke in *okuri ashi barai*.

Ko Uchi Gari

Uke will try to sweep your right foot from the inside. As Uke extends with the right foot to perform the sweep, put your right foot on to the mat and pivot, bringing your back towards Uke, and throw in one of the conventional hip or hand techniques, for example *tai otoshi*.

The counter techniques listed above are only a few which may be used. As you practise the throw, others will be discovered which may work better for you. Judo is very much an individual art, and a technique which suits one player may often be virtually impossible for another player to perform.

The following techniques are some counter moves which I have found to be useful:

Ko soto gari as a counter – As Uke steps in for his throw, Tori places his left foot to the rear of Uke's right ankle.

Tori sweeps Uke's foot across his body in *ko soto gari*.

Uke falls at Tori's side as the counter is completed.

Ko Soto Gari

This is a most useful and powerful technique if performed properly and swiftly. It relies upon Uke being caught in mid-turn with his or her weight on the left foot, and is effective against such throws as *seoi nage*, *ashi guruma*, *o guruma*, *hiki tai* and *hane goshi*.

As Uke's right foot is brought across your front during the turn in, sway your weight on to your right foot. Sweep your left foot across your body and forwards, taking Uke's right leg in *ko soto gari*. This must be done precisely and quickly in order to catch Uke's foot before it touches the mat. Here Laurence effectively counters Ken's *kata seoi* with *ko soto gari*.

Hiza Gaeshi

This is a fairly unconventional move which will only work a few times on your opponent. It relies upon Uke entering without completely unbalancing you in a forward direction, so that you still have flexibility of movement. It is, however, quite spectacular in application whilst being simple. It may be used against such hand/hip throws as *kubi nage*, *tai otoshi*, and so on.

As Uke turns in you step sideways to your right about one foot distant. Slide your left foot towards you so that your left knee is directly behind Uke's right knee. Drop into *jigotai* (defensive) posture, bending your left knee forwards into the back of Uke's knee. Pull to Uke's rear with your left hand on the sleeve to complete the move.

Sukui Nage

This is a throw in its own right which may be adapted for use as a counter. As Uke turns in for a hand throw such as *kubi nage*, or a hip throw such as *tsuri komi goshi*, slide your left hand across the front of Uke's body, reaching for the left armpit. Bend forward, placing your right hand, palm upward, to the rear of either Uke's right or left knee, whichever is most convenient. Turn your body to the left, pushing back with your left arm and lifting with your right to throw Uke to your rear.

COUNTER TWOS

The counter two is a simple combination applying a second throwing technique after you have executed the counter one movement. The first counter must be applied with a minimum of weight transfer and force, so that Uke is not thrown but only unbalanced by your movement. This gives you time to apply a second standing technique from the position you are in. In the case of the basic *sumi otoshi* counter, the second technique is usually *o soto guruma*, *ashi gake* or *o soto otoshi*, these throws being favoured from this position.

From the moment that Uke moves in for the throw, you step to your rear (although not as far as you would in counter one), turning your body to your left. Uke is unbalanced to the

Counter two – As Uke steps in for a throw, Tori steps back as in the counter one.

Instead of transferring her weight back, Tori now steps across the rear of Uke's legs to counter with *o soto guruma*.

rear. With your weight firmly on your left foot, step across Uke to block both legs in *o soto guruma*, or one leg in *ashi gake*, depending on the position of your respective bodies and on your balance. For green belts and above the movement may become *o soto otoshi* when the opportunity presents itself.

Counter twos are a demonstration of your knowledge of the syllabus, your control of Uke and your balance. At the termination of the movement you should be standing in *jigotai*, holding Uke's right sleeve and prepared to finish the technique by *atemi* or *newaza* (techniques performed on the ground). Certain techniques, as with counter ones, will vary from the foregoing description, and these are listed as follows:

Hiza Guruma/Sasae Tsuri Komi Ashi

In the initial counter to both these throws you use *hiza guruma*. From the 'in' position, your weight on your right foot, left foot placed against Uke's knee, you are now required to perform a second technique. Drop your left foot to the mat in front of and between Uke's legs. Transfer your weight to your left foot and pivot on it to your left, bringing your right foot through into *tai otoshi*, *kubi nage* or *obi goshi* to complete the counter two.

Ko Soto Gari

In the counter one you are sweeping Uke's left foot across his or her body with your right. Do not complete the sweep, just take it far enough to unbalance Uke to the left rear corner. Place your right foot on the mat, transferring your weight on to it. As you do this Uke will bring his or her left foot back across the body to regain balance. You are now in a position to perform throws to Uke's rear such as *ashi gake, o soto guruma, ko soto gake* or *o soto otoshi*. The choice of your second technique should be dictated by your position respective to Uke and by your grade.

Harai Tsuri Komi Ashi/Uchi Ashi Gake/O Uchi Gari

The counter one to these throws left you in the position to perform *uchi ashi gake/o uchi gari*. Having taken your right leg around the rear of Uke's calf, do not continue the move any further, but bring your leg back to the left to a position behind Uke's right leg. You can now perform *ko uchi gari* or *uchi ashi sasae* depending on your grade.

De Ashi Barai

The counter one finished with *tai otoshi*. From this position extend your leg back and drop your knee almost to the mat for *koshi guruma* to complete the counter two technique.

Okuri Ashi Barai

From the counter one position of *okuri ashi barai* with your right hand on Uke's belt show a token lift and place your left foot behind Uke's foot to demonstrate the sweep. At this point turn your body to the left, sliding your hand around Uke's waist to the back, and step into *obi goshi* gripping Uke's belt at the back.

Ko Uchi Gari

Your counter one to *ko uchi gari* has finished in a hand or hip technique. It is now a simple move to execute a technique two from this position, such as *te hiza sasae* or *kata seoi*.

The technique of counter twos can now be seen as the application of the simple technique two (combination technique) in a counter situation. Theoretically it would be possible to perform counter threes, fours, and so on. However, the syllabus does not require such movements. These counters are quite useful ways of teaching the syllabus and may be tried at will.

COUNTER TWO-BY-TWOS

This is a complicated demonstration which is introduced at orange to green stage. It simulates the advanced *randori* which may be practised by some Dan grades in which they counter one another until one makes a mistake and is thrown. The basic principle is that the person who initiates the first throw is Uke, who is finally thrown by Tori. The following steps are performed in counter two-by-twos:

(a) Uke steps in to perform a normal throw.
(b) Tori performs a counter to this throw but is not successful in throwing Uke.
(c) Uke then counters Tori's counter but is not able to throw.
(d) Tori performs a further counter and completes the demonstration by successfully throwing Uke.

There are certain points which should be borne in mind when performing these demonstrations:

(1) The use of the same counter twice by either player is to be discouraged. In this demonstration the players are expected to exhibit their knowledge of the syllabus and the mat experience they have gained.
(2) Turning from right-hand techniques to left-hand techniques is also discouraged. However, where little else can be done this is permissible.
(3) This is a demonstration and should be performed in a smooth and unhurried manner. No marks are given for swift but sloppy technique.
(4) The secret of this technique is to turn well around your partner, the counters being circular in motion. A change in direction is often the signal for the final throwing technique.

It is not possible to demonstrate these movements in print; they must be performed under the guidance of a qualified Zen instructor so that they may be fully appreciated and learned.

The counters demonstrated in this chapter are by no means exhaustive, and most instructors will have other techniques which they favour. Many of these may well be better and more effective than those I have described. However the foregoing is the aggregate of many years of experience under the tuition of some of the best technical players in the Zen Judo Family, and represents the more common techniques used in Zen Judo today.

6
SACRIFICE TECHNIQUES

The term 'sacrifice' in Judo describes the act of abandoning your strong posture on your feet in order to carry out the throw. These movements are categorised into side sacrifices (*yokosutemiwaza*) and back sacrifices (*masutemiwaza*). Sacrifice techniques are taught from orange belt upwards, and at green belt you will begin to encounter full sacrifice techniques. For orange belts a partial technique is taught, called the half-sacrifice.

Thirteen full sacrifices are required to be demonstrated for the black belt grading, and the syllabus which follows describes the thirteen which are taught. This chapter is broken down by types of sacrifice, and the full sacrifice section into the order of the syllabus. The first section of the full sacrifices contains three basic movements to the side and back and is required for green to blue grading. The second section shows another four techniques which will enable the student to demonstrate sufficient mastery of *sutemiwaza* for the grading to 1st Kyu (brown belt). The final section lists the remaining six *sutemi* required for black belt.

It is essential that the student can not only perform these techniques but is also not nervous of them. From personal experience I am aware that this is probably one of the most difficult barriers for many students to cross along the road to their black belts, and the manner in which these sacrifices are taught initially is crucial. Everybody has a different personality, and many people who take up Zen Judo do so because they wish to overcome a timid nature and gain self-confidence. For many, myself included, the thought of being thrown in this way can be quite frightening and it may take weeks or months to become accustomed to it.

Zen Judo is an art for everyone to enjoy, and should cater for the majority, male and female alike, rather than for the minority who only attend for competitive sport. With this in mind I make no apologies for devoting so much of this chapter to the manner in which I feel that sacrifice techniques should be taught. I was unfortunate enough to have been subjected to several humiliating lessons in these techniques which nearly ruined my confidence at green belt stage, so I have endeavoured to formulate teaching methods which help to build up confidence rather than demolish it.

GRADED INSTRUCTION

The newly graded green belt is required to take several lessons in *sutemi* early on, as all persons who are wearing this colour are expected to be able to take these throws after a few weeks. The first lesson is particularly important as this will set the scene for those which follow. For many students the concept of diving over Tori is almost as bad as being thrown over Tori. This is the reason why such exercises are practised from the first week the student commences training on the mat.

The simplest way to begin this instruction is not by expecting the students to perform such movements as *yoko wakare* or *sumi gaeshi*, but to start with counter sacrifice techniques. Uke throws Tori in a simple technique (*kubi nage* or *tai otoshi*) with Tori keeping hold throughout the throw. When Tori lands Uke is pulled over Tori in a sacrifice counter. This is a relatively simple technique which may commence with Tori gently pulling until Uke dives over. This will soon build up to a full sacrifice counter as confidence is gained.

Whilst the syllabus specifies the three sacrifices to be learned for the next grading, the simplest *sutemi* to commence with is *yoko gake* as a standing technique. Again, this can be started on the basis of mutual co-operation and built up from there. *Korobi sutemi* is yet another simple move which will get Uke to roll over Tori. These techniques should be practised until the student has gained confidence.

The teaching for *tomoe nage* can be quite difficult and I would advise instructors to perform this throw with each student, acting as Uke. In this way you can ensure that each student performs the throw correctly before practising on the other students. There is nothing more worrying than being forced to practise with a fellow student who throws you incorrectly. Similarly, I insist upon my instructors performing *tomoe nage* upon the students themselves until they have gained confidence with the throw. Happily, *tomoe nage* has been promoted to the blue to brown syllabus so it is not quite as important for the green belt to learn quickly. *Sumi gaeshi*, however, is a similar throw and the same method would apply when teaching this technique.

By instructing in this manner I have found that I do not lose many students at this stage. This may appear to some to be an over-sensitive approach to *sutemi* instruction, but it is far better to nurse the student across a hurdle than to run a club with a high drop-out rate or injury record.

HALF-SACRIFICE TECHNIQUES

These are initially taught once the student has attained orange belt. The half-sacrifice technique entails Tori dropping to one knee whilst executing the throw. Half-sacrifices can be applied to the majority of standing techniques, the exception being the foot sweeps. The orange to green syllabus requires only four half-sacrifices, and I shall describe these. Most other throws can be adapted to this basic method, and the higher grading syllabus extends the range of half-sacrifices required. These techniques must be practised to the left as well as to the right.

Ashi gake half-sacrifice – Tori steps forward with his left foot and drops to his right knee to complete the ashi gake.

Kubi Nage Half-Sacrifice

Tori moves in to perform *kubi nage* as described earlier, but when the throw is commenced you pivot upon the ball of your right foot and the heel of your left. Pivoting to your left, you drop your right knee to the mat to assist the throw, Uke being deposited on the mat in front of you.

The nature of the throw means that Uke will travel to the mat with more force, and it is important that Uke can breakfall well before this is practised. This is the reason why the half-sacrifices do not appear until the student has gained some experience.

Ashi Gake Half-Sacrifice

This simple move is usually the first of this group to be taught. You step to Uke's right side, bringing your right foot through and behind Uke's right ankle into *ashi gake*. As you step forward with your left foot, drop to your right knee, Uke falling beside you in left breakfall.

Kubi nage half-sacrifice – Tori turns to her left and drops to her right knee to perform this half-sacrifice.

Tai Otoshi Half-Sacrifice

Move into *tai otoshi* as described previously. As you throw, pivot on your feet as described in the *kubi nage* half-sacrifice above, dropping to your right knee. This is a slightly more comfortable throw to perform as your feet are wider apart and there is consequently less height to drop from.

When the student is well versed in the half-sacrifice techniques and can breakfall naturally, a second version of the throw is taught. This is the *tai otoshi* half-sacrifice on the left knee. This does not imply a left-hand throw, but a version where you step across Uke with your right foot to outside Uke's right foot, pulling Uke forward to break his or her balance. Instead of stepping back with your left foot you turn your body to the left, bending your left leg at the knee and landing on it. Your right leg is stretched across Uke's shins and you pull Uke over this leg to complete a very fast *tai otoshi*.

Tai otoshi half-sacrifice – This technique must be performed very quickly and Uke's balance properly broken forwards before attempting it.

Kata Seoi Half-Sacrifice

This technique is similar to the others described where Tori pivots, turns and drops to the right knee as the throw is executed. Because of the position of the fulcrum point – Uke's right shoulder – Uke will tend to hit the mat with more force than normal, so some care should be taken at first with this technique.

All the other half-sacrifices in the syllabus take the form of the throws so far described. Some will be more effective than others, depending on the fulcrum point relative to Uke's centre of gravity, such as *hiki tai* which is a very hard and fast throw when performed this way.

FULL SACRIFICE TECHNIQUES

GREEN TO BLUE BELT SYLLABUS

Yoko Wakare

Lift-pull with both hands to break Uke's balance forwards. Turn your right side towards Uke and drop on to your left side immediately in front of Uke, both feet sliding past to Uke's right. Your legs are now blocking Uke's advance so that your pull as you fall will cause Uke to somersault over your waist into a right rolling breakfall.

This technique makes an effective counter to many hip throws if you step quickly round in front of Uke and fall with a forward pull.

Yoko wakare

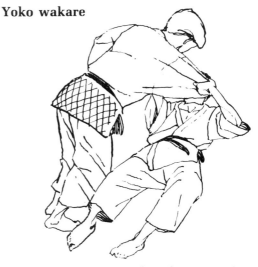

Yoko wakare – Note the position of both Tori's legs. Uke is being drawn over Tori to make a rolling breakfall.

Uki Waza

This is a delicate technique which may require careful timing for its proper execution. Pull Uke forwards with both hands. Lightly extend your left leg and throw yourself on to your left side. Your right leg extends beyond Uke's legs while Uke floats over your outstretched left leg into a right rolling breakfall.

Uki waza – Not dissimilar to *yoko wakare*, Uke is drawn over the outstretched left leg of Tori.

Uki waza

Sumi Gaeshi

This useful technique can be adapted to many situations and may be performed with the minimum of effort on the part of Tori. *Sumi gaeshi* is especially suited to counter the defensive *jigotai* posture adopted by many players.

Sumi gaeshi

Sumi gaeshi – Uke is thrown over Tori's left shoulder. Note the position of Tori's right foot which raises Uke's left thigh to help execute the throw.

Place your right hand under Uke's left armpit and around the back. With your left hand pull Uke's right sleeve tightly against your left side. Your left foot is placed midway between Uke's legs and behind Uke's heels as you fall back, raising your right leg to place your right instep against the inside of Uke's left knee or slightly higher. Uke's left leg is lifted up by your right foot as you pull down with your left hand and lift with your right. Uke is thrown over your left shoulder to land in a right rolling breakfall.

BLUE TO BROWN BELT SYLLABUS

Tomoe Nage

This is the most important of the *masutemi* group of throws, and is the most spectacular. It is not a throw to be undertaken without considerable practice, and students may need a slow build-up before they can confidently be taken over with it. The use of a soft crash mat is often employed to help the student gain confidence from this throw.

Tomoe nage

Tomoe nage – Note the position of Tori's legs as he commences the throw.

Using both hands, lift-pull Uke forwards, sliding your left foot between Uke's legs and raising your right foot to place the sole just below Uke's navel. Fall backwards as you do this, pulling Uke over you. Straighten your right leg and pull with both hands to throw Uke directly over your head. Uke should land with a right rolling breakfall.

Yoko Guruma

This sacrifice technique utilises a change in direction and a blending with Uke's line of resistance. Step in with your left foot to the rear of Uke's right, turning towards Uke. Your feet are placed one in front and one to the rear of Uke. Clasp Uke around the waist at belt level with both hands. As Uke leans forward in response to the throw that appears to be coming, slide your right foot deeply between Uke's legs and fall onto your side to throw Uke over your left shoulder into a rolling breakfall.

Tani Otoshi

When performed well this technique has the effect of sweeping Uke's legs forward and can result in quite a heavy throw. The sacrifice may be completed in two ways. The first is used when the student is inexperienced in sutemi, whilst the second can be utilised on the move.

Tani otoshi

(a) Step forward with your right foot outside Uke's right foot. Pivot on the ball of your right foot, bringing your left foot around to the rear of Uke's left foot. Fall back, pulling Uke down with you and sweeping Uke's legs away from the rear. Both of you should land simultaneously with right and left breakfalls respectively.

(b) Slide your left foot deeply outside Uke's right, your left knee reaching to the same point as Uke's right ankle. Put your right hand under Uke's left armpit and pull with your left hand on Uke's right sleeve. Fall on to your left side, throwing Uke over your outstretched left leg to the rear of your left shoulder.

Towara Gaeshi

From a *jigotai* position Uke reaches over to grasp your belt at the rear, intending to roll you over. Raise your right arm and circle it around Uke's neck, trapping Uke's head under your right armpit. Slide your right foot between Uke's legs, catching Uke's right leg with your left hand and roll Uke over your right shoulder.

BROWN TO BLACK BELT SYLLABUS

Yoko Gake

This is a simple sacrifice technique which may be completed in two ways. The first method is for demonstration of the standing technique, whilst the second method is for use during *randori*.

(a) Step forward with your right foot outside Uke's right foot. Pivot on the ball of your right foot, turning so that your left foot is placed against the rear of Uke's right heel. Pull Uke's right sleeve to the rear with your left hand and fall to the mat pulling Uke down with you. Both of you should land and breakfall simultaneously, Uke with a left and Tori with a right breakfall.

Yoko gake

(b) Pull on Uke's right sleeve to make Uke advance the right foot. As this happens put the sole of your left foot to the side of Uke's right and fall backwards on to your left side. As you are falling continue to pull with your left hand whilst pushing with your right hand to turn Uke on to his or her back. At the same time you are sweeping Uke's right foot across from right to left. If you keep close contact with Uke, you will land close enough to lead into a groundhold.

Yoko Otoshi

This can be likened to a frontal version of *yoko gake*, in which you are pulling Uke into a left breakfall over your falling body. Pull down on Uke's right sleeve, lifting the left lapel to break Uke's balance to the right. Slide your left foot to just outside Uke's right ankle and fall on to your left side. Using your hands, pull Uke over your leg and turn Uke on to his or her back, taking care not to bring Uke down on to the right shoulder, as this could cause injury.

Ura Nage

This is one of the most difficult of the back sacrifices to perform, and Uke needs to be well experienced before you attempt it. Two methods are given, the first being the technique as performed in *nage no kata* whilst the second is for demonstration.

(a) Step in with your left foot to the rear of Uke's right foot, facing Uke's right side as in *yoko guruma*. With your knees bent catch Uke round the waist, your left arm around the back of Uke's waist and your right hand on the front of Uke's stomach. Bend backwards and straighten your knees, lifting Uke clear of the mat. Throw yourself backwards, hurling Uke over your left shoulder. Let go with your left arm as you do this so Uke can land with a rolling breakfall.

(b) An alternative method of accomplishing this throw is when Uke aims a blow at your head. Slip under the fist, thrusting your left foot well to Uke's rear so that the blow passes across your left shoulder. Drop your hips and circle your left arm around Uke's hips. Place your right foot inside Uke's right and apply your right palm, fingers pointing up, to Uke's lower abdomen. Bend back and throw yourself straight backwards, taking Uke over your left shoulder.

Korobi Sutemi

Uke attempts to throw you with *ryo ashi dori*, bending down in front of you to grasp your ankles. Grip Uke's belt at the back with your left hand whilst your right arm passes over Uke's head to protect it from injury. Bring your right arm up under Uke's left armpit as you roll backwards. Keep your head over to your right shoulder whilst rolling Uke over your left shoulder.

Soto maki komi

Soto Maki Komi

This is the basic *maki komi* move, of which there are several versions. One other version is contained within this syllabus, *hane maki komi*. Take your left foot back and place it in front of Uke's left foot. Let go with your right hand, taking your right arm over Uke's right arm. Place your right leg outside Uke's right leg in a *tai otoshi* position. With the combined pull of your left hand and push of your right arm, trap Uke's right arm under your armpit. Turning your body to the left, put your right hand on to the mat and fall on to your right side. Uke is wound over your body to fall beside you.

Hane Maki Komi

Turn in as above, trapping Uke's right arm under your right armpit. Bend your right leg and put it across Uke's legs as in *hane goshi*. Holding Uke tight against your right side, continue turning and put your right hand on to the mat, rolling on to your right side. Uke is whipped over your body to land beside you.

Hane maki komi – Tori is spinning Uke over his bent leg as he performs this sacrifice.

SACRIFICE COUNTERS

There are many versions of counter technique which involve sacrifices, but they generally appear to fall into two distinct groups. The first group is where you have been thrown but retain hold to pull Uke over into a rolling breakfall. These may not technically be classed as sacrifices because you appear to have been thrown by Uke, whether or not you have actually permitted the throw. The second group is where you perform a sacrifice technique as Uke enters for the throw. The movements in this group are the true sacrifice counters.

Within the Zen grading syllabus no differentiation is made between these two groups of techniques and all will count as sacrifice counters. I will therefore discuss them under the same general heading but will group the movements separately.

GROUP 1

These techniques are usually performed to hip or hand throws such as *tai otoshi*, *uki goshi* or *seoi nage*. Whichever throw is performed, the basic movement is the same, so I shall describe just one version which can be adapted to the range of throws.

Sacrifice counter – Tori permits herself to be thrown, retaining hold as the throw is executed. Tori's position as she lands enables her to perform *yoko wakare* upon Uke as a counter throw.

Tai Otoshi/Sacrifice Counter

Uke executes *tai otoshi* in whatever way is most convenient. You retain your grip on Uke's sleeve and collar as you are thrown. As you land do not attempt to breakfall, but pull down on Uke's collar and sleeve to bend Uke forwards. Roll to your left, pulling Uke over you. Uke performs a rolling breakfall over your body.

It is advisable to ensure that Uke initiates the dive over Tori when both are inexperienced. Tori should let go of Uke's sleeve at the point of the dive and of the collar just as Uke is going over. On no account should Tori pull Uke over on to the right shoulder as this may result in injury. Once this technique has been practised thoroughly it can be performed in a fast and spectacular manner and is a useful movement for demonstration purposes.

GROUP 2

Tai Otoshi/Tani Otoshi

Uke moves in for *tai otoshi* in the normal manner. As Uke turns in, slide your left foot across and to the rear of Uke's left foot, pushing it forward. Throw yourself backwards into *tani otoshi*, pulling Uke down at the same time. This move can be utilised for most of the hand or hip throws which involve Uke turning in to you.

Uki Goshi/Yoko Guruma

As Uke turns in for *uki goshi*, you step round with your right foot to Uke's front. Slide your right foot deep between Uke's legs, turning to Uke's front to land and pull Uke over your left shoulder into a rolling breakfall.

Counter sacrifice to uki goshi – Uke turns in to perform *uki goshi.*

Tori spins on his left foot, bringing his right foot around to Uke's front and between Uke's legs.

Tori continues his turn, falling on to his side to perform the counter sacrifice *yoko guruma.*

Ko Soto Gake/Sumi Gaeshi

Sumi gaeshi may be utilised for sacrifice counter purposes to most of the forward moving throws such as *ashi gake, ko uchi maki komi,* and so on. As Uke moves in for *ko soto gake,* slide your left foot forwards and fall on to your back. Your right instep may be utilised to help take Uke over your left shoulder into *sumi gaeshi.*

By varying your techniques between the four general movements described above in both groups, you will be able to effect a suitable counter sacrifice to every throw in the syllabus. With *ryo ashi dori* you would utilise *korobi sutemi* as a counter, as described previously.

Counter sacrifice to ko soto gake – Uke enters to perform ko soto gake.

Tori commences to fall backwards, holding on to Uke.

Tori performs *sumi gaeshi* counter sacrifice upon Uke.

SACRIFICE TWOS AND THREES

This seemingly small section of the Zen syllabus is a combination of the performance of technique twos and threes (twos for blue to brown, threes for brown to black) to finish with a sacrifice technique. In the sacrifice twos, the second technique must be the sacrifice, whilst with the sacrifice threes you perform a technique two followed by a recognised full sacrifice technique.

Kubi Nage/Ko Uchi Maki Komi/Uki Waza

This combination would be classed as a sacrifice three from *kubi nage*. Having turned in to perform *kubi nage*, you then change to a technique two into *ko uchi maki komi* by sliding your right foot through Uke's legs to block Uke's right foot at the rear. Your left hand drops to Uke's right knee and you turn half-way round to partly face Uke. Theoretically Uke realises that you are about to throw to the rear and so resists to the front. You now extend your left foot across Uke's body and fall on to your back into *uki waza*. You may assist the sacrifice by lifting Uke's left leg with your right instep.

Ko Soto Gake/Sumi Gaeshi

This is a sacrifice two from *ko soto gake*. As you enter *ko soto gake* do not lean too heavily on Uke. As Uke resists your forward movement, slide your left foot forward, dropping down on to your back and bringing your right instep into contact with Uke's left inner thigh. Throw Uke over your left shoulder in *sumi gaeshi*.

Seoi Nage/Yoko Wakare

This sacrifice two to *seoi nage*, or to most of the other hip techniques, utilises a side sacrifice for better control. Having turned in for *seoi nage*, throw your legs to Uke's right side and drop down so that your seat is roughly in line with Uke's left foot. Pull Uke forward over you into *yoko wakare*.

Kubi nage sacrifice three – Tori enters to perform kubi nage.

Tori changes his technique to ko uchi maki komi.

Tori completes the combination with uki waza or yoko otoshi for a sacrifice three.

Soto gake sacrifice two –
Tori enters to perform soto gake.

Tori spins on his right foot,
starting to fall to his left.

Tori completes the sacrifice two
with yoko gake.

Soto Gake/Yoko Gake

A simple sacrifice two to *soto gake*, or *ko soto gake*, is performed by turning your body, with your left foot on the mat blocking Uke's right heel at the rear. Pivot on your left foot, pulling Uke backwards into *yoko gake*.

O Guruma/Tai Otoshi/Yoko Wakare

This sacrifice three to *o guruma* incorporates a simple technique two to *o guruma*. *Tai otoshi* follows naturally, and it is a simple matter to step across with your left foot, thus allowing yourself to fall into *yoko wakare*.

It is self-evident that many further combinations may be practised, according to your preference. The above are merely descriptions of some which can be adopted, and they are by no means exclusive or exhaustive. Neither would I be so dogmatic as to state that these are the ideal combinations; they just happen to suit my stature and personal style. Every student will discover techniques which suit their physical abilities, and movements which feel natural should be encouraged where possible.

HALF-SACRIFICE TWOS AND THREES

These consist of a technique two (or three), the final technique being completed by a half-sacrifice. It is important to bear in mind that your final technique should be one which lends itself to a half-sacrifice. Certain techniques cannot be readily utilised as half-sacrifices without difficulty and should be avoided, such *hiza guruma, ashi guruma* and the foot-sweep techniques.

Examples of these half-sacrifice two and three techniques are:

Half-Sacrifice Twos

    (1) Kubi nage/tai otoshi half-sacrifice.
    (2) *Hiza guruma/uki goshi* half-sacrifice.
    (3) *O guruma/obi goshi* half-sacrifice.
    (4) *Ko uchi gari/uki goshi* half-sacrifice.

Half-Sacrifice Threes

    (1) *O uchi gari/ko uchi gari/uki goshi* half-sacrifice.
    (2) *Uchi mata/ko tsuri goshi/tai otoshi* half-sacrifice.
    (3) *O soto gari/o soto guruma/ashi gake* half-sacrifice.
    (4) *Hane goshi/obi goshi/uki goshi* half-sacrifice.

The performance of these specialised combinations within the grading syllabus is only for demonstration purposes and therefore they should not be attempted at full speed. It is wise to try to avoid the speed/accuracy trade-off and concentrate upon good technique rather than swiftness of movement.

Practice of these combinations is intended to instil the knowledge that a technique which may be applied slightly incorrectly during *randori* will often succeed if turned into a half-sacrifice, full sacrifice or a technique two. With the half-sacrifice it is always the right knee (left knee for left-handed technique) that is used with such combinations as are given above. The opposite knee half-sacrifice is quite difficult to apply within a combination technique.

Considerable ground has been covered in this chapter and a wealth of detail has been given. It is intended that this book will be used as a manual for many students, so complete understanding of all that has been included within this chapter is not expected.

Apart from being of instructional interest to Zen students, I hope that this text will be of some interest to players from differing styles. It should at least give an insight into our style and syllabus, and may help dispel many of the erroneous opinions held by those who prefer muscle to technique.

7
GROUNDHOLDS

Groundwork (*newaza*) may be classified into three separate sections: firstly the methods of holding Uke down on the ground (*osaekomiwaza*); secondly the techniques of holding Uke in a neck-lock or stranglehold (*shimewaza*); and finally the various bone or joint-locks (*kansetsuwaza*).

There is little doubt that where a good throw may fail to deter a strong antagonist, or you find yourself with insufficient space to perform a throw, knowledge of the techniques of *newaza*, especially the latter two subdivisions, may well save your life. Unfortunately the techniques under the headings of *shimewaza* and *kansetsuwaza* can be very dangerous or even lethal, so Kyu grades in the Zen Judo Family are not normally instructed in these until they are ready for Dan grade.

This chapter will therefore be devoted only to *osaekomiwaza*, the rest of the *newaza* syllabus being left for another volume aimed at training after 1st Dan. The syllabus requires all potential Dan grades to be familiar with twelve separate hold-down techniques. These are specified within each syllabus and are listed below in the order that they should be taught.

LIST OF GROUNDHOLDS

White–yellow belt: *kesa gatame*
                    kazure kesa gatame
Yellow–orange belt: *kata gatame*
                    makura kesa gatame
Orange–green belt: *ushiro (gyaku) kesa gatame*
                    mune gatame
Green–blue belt: *yoko shiho gatame*
                    kazure yoko shiho gatame
Blue–brown belt: *kazure kami shiho gatame*
                    tate shiho gatame
Brown–black belt: *kami shiho gatame*
                    kazure tate shiho gatame

Kesa Gatame (Scarf Hold)

This is the most basic and simplest of the groundholds, which has several close variations. You must remember to hold your head down when putting this technique on and grip Uke's gi firmly. Uke's right arm must be tightly trapped between your left arm and your body.

Kesa gatame

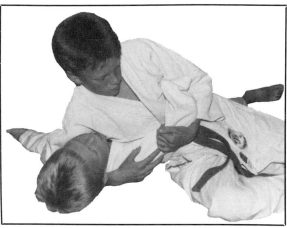

Kesa gatame – Note that Tori is sitting up to demonstrate the hold more clearly. Tori's left hand is in an alternative position from that usually encountered.

With Uke lying flat, sit down at Uke's right side. Take hold of Uke's gi at the right shoulder with your left hand and trap Uke's right arm under your armpit. Bring your right knee forwards under Uke's right arm and extend your left leg out at right angles to Uke's body. Circle Uke's neck with your right arm, bringing your hip up into the solar plexus and relaxing your weight on to Uke. Grasp the back of Uke's collar with your right hand, keeping your head forwards and to the left of Uke's head. Relax your body when Uke struggles.

Kazure Kesa Gatame (Broken Scarf Hold)

This is the first hold in the *kata* of ground work that you will eventually have to perform for grading to third Dan, *katame no kata*, so all students must be familiar with it. There are two versions as described below:

With Uke lying flat, sit at Uke's right side. Take hold of the gi at the right shoulder with your left hand and trap Uke's right arm under your armpit. Bring your right knee forwards under Uke's right arm and extend your left leg at right angles to Uke's body.

(a) Slide your right arm between Uke's left arm and body, bringing your right hand up behind Uke's left shoulder. Grasp the gi under Uke's left shoulder and rest your weight across Uke, lifting the shoulders off the mat; or

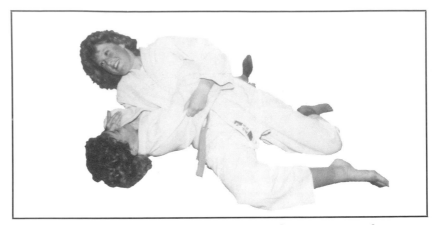

Kazure kesa gatame – Note Tori's position leaning over Uke's chest and the right hand under Uke's shoulder.

(b) Trap Uke's left arm under your right armpit in the same fashion as the other arm and grasp the *gi* under the left shoulder. Bring your right leg further forwards beyond Uke's right shoulder. Rest your right hip on Uke and your weight across him or her, lifting the shoulders off the mat.

Kata Gatame (Shoulder Hold)

This hold tends to strangle your opponent, making for effective immobilisation as it traps Uke's right arm in the process. Remember that your hands are clenched together rather than holding the *gi*.

Kata gatame

Push Uke's right arm with your left hand on the elbow, driving it across Uke's throat. Bring your head down behind Uke's right elbow and catch hold of your right hand with your left. Pull your right arm up with your left hand and put your forehead on the mat, pressing Uke's arm to the side of Uke's head. Hold tight and move around with Uke during the struggle, keeping your body relaxed.

Makura Kesa Gatame (Pillow Cross-Chest Hold)

This technique is a recent addition to the Zen syllabus and introduces a hold from a different angle. It is important that you wrap yourself around Uke so that you can lean your weight on to Uke's chest to pin Uke down.

Makura kesa gatame

Slide your left arm under Uke's right armpit from behind and bring your left knee up under the back of Uke's head. Clasp both hands together and lean over Uke's chest. By making a pillow with your left thigh you ensure that Uke cannot bridge to release the hold.

Ushiro Kesa Gatame (Rear Cross-Chest Hold)

This hold can be extremely effective when your weight is placed over Uke's head. Uke's left arm may lie either under Tori's left elbow or over it – either variation is permissible.

With Uke lying flat, face Uke's feet sitting on the right side above his or her shoulders. Place your left arm over (or under) Uke's left arm, bringing the elbow down on to Uke's left upper arm and holding the *gi* or the belt to keep the elbow in place. Take your right arm over Uke's right arm and pin it under your right armpit. Relax your weight across Uke's chest.

Mune Gatame (Chest Hold)

This can be an effective hold, relying on trapping Uke's body between your right elbow and right knee. It follows the previous hold by a simple movement and is easy to maintain.

With Uke lying flat, kneel facing Uke's right side and lean across the body. Grasp Uke's left sleeve under the arm with your right hand, putting your elbow against Uke's left hip. Pass your left arm over Uke's body and place your elbow on the mat above Uke's left shoulder. Catch Uke's belt with your left hand passing under the left shoulder. Keep your right

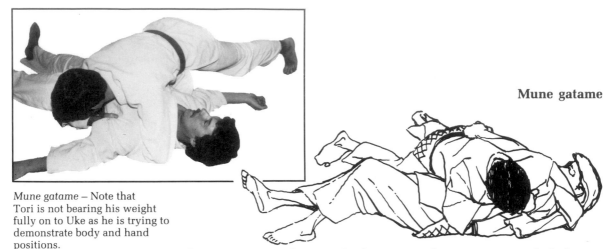

Mune gatame

Mune gatame – Note that Tori is not bearing his weight fully on to Uke as he is trying to demonstrate body and hand positions.

knee against Uke's right hip, stretching out your left leg to your rear with the toes into the mat. Uke's hips are thus pressed firmly between your right knee and right elbow, preventing Uke from turning. Relax all your weight on to Uke to effect the hold.

Yoko Shiho Gatame (Side Locking Four-Quarters Hold)

This is the basic side holding, and other variations in use only build upon this position. Considerable strength is needed to maintain this hold when Uke is struggling.

With Uke lying flat kneel at Uke's right side, passing your left hand under Uke's head to catch hold of the gi at the left shoulder and pull Uke's shoulders to the mat. Bring your right arm between Uke's legs and grasp the rear skirt of Uke's jacket or the belt (*obi*) if you can reach it. Lie forwards across Uke's body with your head on Uke's left side, relaxing all your weight to hold Uke down. Stretch your legs wide apart with toes into the mat, taking as little weight as possible on toes or elbows.

Yoko shiho gatame – Again Tori is not fully into position so that you can see the hand positions.

Kazure Yoko Shiho Gatame
(Broken Side Locking Four-Quarters Hold)

This follows from the previous hold when Uke manages to break your grip on the *gi*, and can be a more effective hold. A permissible variation is to remove your right arm from between Uke's legs and slide it under Uke's body to grasp the left sleeve, thus holding Uke's left arm to his or her side. If you push your left elbow to the ground and bear your weight on to your left upper arm you can effect a strangle upon Uke at the same time.

Kazure yoko shiho gatame

Kneel at Uke's side, as in the previous hold. Pass your left hand over Uke's throat and round the left shoulder to grasp Uke's belt at the rear. Pass your right hand between Uke's legs and grasp the rear skirt of the *gi*. Lie forwards across Uke's body with your head to Uke's left side, relaxing all your weight to hold Uke down. Stretch your legs wide apart with your toes into the mat, taking as little weight as possible on toes or elbows.

Kazure Kami Shiho Gatame
(Broken Upper Four-Quarters Hold)

This hold follows naturally from the last one if you retain the grip with your left hand and slide to the top of Uke's body. Remember to get Uke's head to turn to one side before performing this hold.

Kazure kami shiho gatame

Kneel to the rear of Uke's head looking towards the feet. Pass your left arm under Uke's left shoulder and grasp the belt at the left side, pulling it down to the mat. Pass your right arm over Uke's right shoulder and under Uke's right arm to grasp the collar at the rear of Uke's neck. Trap Uke's right arm to your right side with your elbow. Spread your legs and lower your body to put your chin on Uke's stomach. Your stomach tends to be over Uke's left shoulder rather than over Uke's face.

Tate Shiho Gatame (Straight Locking Four-Quarters Hold)

Your action in this hold can cause Uke some pain when applied with power as it also acts as a leg lock. This would not be allowed in competition but could be a useful immobilisation technique.

Tate shiho gatame – This shows Tori's position, including the foot entanglement.

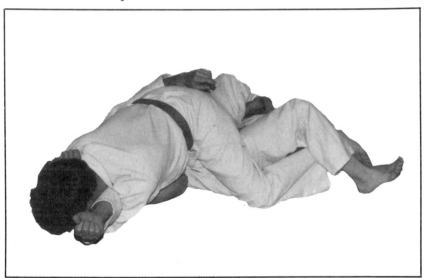

With Uke lying flat with knees raised and feet on the mat, kneel astride and tuck your feet around Uke's legs from the outside to catch the inside of the calves. Raise Uke's right arm above his or her head and fold your arms around Uke's head and arm, bringing your forearms under the head. Take your head forwards to the mat whilst your folded arms are trapping Uke's right arm to the side of your head. Relax your weight on to Uke.

Kami Shiho Gatame (Upper Four-Quarters Hold)

This is a less effective hold than many of the others but it is included because it is part of *katame no kata*. Its use in demonstration of groundholds is as a pure technique, but its application requires Tori to be much heavier and stronger than Uke for its success.

With Uke lying flat, kneel to the rear of Uke's head facing the feet. Pass your hands under Uke's shoulders to catch the belt at either side of Uke's body. Pull the belt at both sides down to the mat, holding Uke down with the pressure. Bring your body forwards with your chin on Uke's stomach and spread your legs wide apart with toes into the mat. Lower your stomach on to Uke's head (Uke will turn to one side), relaxing your weight on to Uke.

Kazure Tate Shiho Gatame
(Broken Straight Locking Four-Quarters Hold)

This final technique releases Uke's head and left arm, transferring your weight across the body more than lengthways.

Uke lies flat with knees bent and feet on the mat whilst you kneel astride, locking your legs as in *tate shiho gatame*. Pass your right hand over Uke's right shoulder and down the back to grasp the belt. Your left hand passes under Uke's right armpit and around Uke's right upper arm to grip your own collar at the front. Lower your body across Uke towards the right side, keeping your feet tucked under Uke's legs.

The secret of success in all groundwork is to keep your body as low as you can, relaxing so that you press as much weight as possible on to Uke. To ensure this you try not to support yourself with either knees or elbows.

With sufficient knowledge, Uke may be able to escape easily from most of these holds, and there are several standard moves for escape from each one. There are also means of countering these escapes as well. Some of the more common ones are described as follows:

Kesa Gatame/Kazure Kesa Gatame/Kata Gatame

(1) Uke tries to sit up – countered by moving your left foot back towards Uke's feet.
(2) Uke lifts the hips to try to buck you over his or her head – countered by crossing your left leg over your right and pushing your weight back down.
(3) Uke grasps your belt and tries to roll you over – countered by putting your right hand on the mat to push yourself back.

Makura Kesa Gatame/Ushiro Kesa Gatame

(1) Uke attempts to free his or her head or one of the trapped arms — countered by moving with Uke to maintain your relative positions.

Mune Gatame/Yoko Shiho Gatame/Kazure Yoko Shiho Gatame

(1) Uke attempts to roll to the left – countered by placing your hand on the mat and pushing back.
(2) Uke bridges and tries to turn towards your direction – countered by dropping your weight fully on to Uke and pulling in with your arms.
(3) Uke may try to push your head down and hook it with the left leg – countered by keeping your head up towards Uke's left shoulder. If this fails, put your head down to the ground near Uke's left thigh. If Uke manages to hook a leg over your head, let go with your right hand and bring that arm back towards your body, turning away from Uke's direction into *kami shiho gatame* position.

Kami and Kazure Kami Shiho Gatame

(1) Uke moves round in order to try to sit up – countered by moving with Uke so that your bodies are always in a straight line.
(2) Uke bridges, grasps your belt and drops one leg through the gap made by this bridge in order to turn over into the same hold – countered by pulling down strongly on the side that Uke tries to raise and extending the opposite foot.

Tate and Kazure Tate Shiho Gatame

(1) Uke attempts to turn you over – countered by extending one leg in the direction of this turn.

As I have stated previously, the grappling techniques of *osaekomiwaza* do not feature highly in the Zen syllabus or in the actual gradings. This part of the grading will consist mainly of demonstrating the named groundholds for your particular syllabus, and you may be asked for one of the holds to be contested by Uke. This is certainly insufficient motivation for students to specialise in methods of escape and counter whilst on the ground.

From my personal knowledge, many Zen players do not like groundwork and have chosen to attend our classes because of this. Certainly the majority of women who study Zen Judo have little interest in groundwork and will only learn the holds out of necessity. *Newaza* is thus taught as a method of immobilisation of an opponent rather than as a method of fighting.

There are many who will say 'How can you have Judo without groundwork?' However the popularity of most Zen clubs speaks for itself. I originally introduced an element of competition into my club at all levels, with one evening per month being devoted to this. After about two years the number of senior contestants could be counted on the fingers of one hand. If Zen Judo were based upon competitive gradings with this type of training at all sessions, I would not have more than a handful of seniors, unlike the matful that I have now.

This chapter has been devoted to the basics of groundwork, and the escapes and counters are by no means exhaustive. This section of Judo could well be the subject of a separate book itself. The serious student is advised to learn the holds carefully in the order they are presented here, and to know them by name. This way there will be no problems with this section of the grading.

8
GRADINGS

This chapter is written for the benefit of both the person conducting the grading and the students being graded. The techniques of grading are quite simple but easily overlooked, and the experienced grader must pay attention to several aspects of the student's performance before coming to a final decision. On the other hand, it will be of great use to the student to understand what the grader will be looking for, and this knowledge may make the difference between a bare pass and a good pass.

The grader expects the student to come to a grading with a good overall knowledge of the syllabus for the belt that he or she is trying for. It is obvious lack of, or gaps in, this knowledge that will cause failure. No grader likes to fail students, and it gives the grader satisfaction when the students are good and all techniques are performed correctly without undue hesitation. Certain allowances are made during the session for nerves on the part of the student – one cannot expect less – and lapses due to a nervous disposition are tolerated as long as they do not hold up the grading unduly.

PREPARING FOR GRADING

The student must be thoroughly conversant with the syllabus. This comes only from practice, not only on the mat but mentally as well. When I go for a grading I mentally rehearse each throw every day for at least a fortnight beforehand. I make sure that I know every throw that will be asked of me, and where two or three throws could be mixed up I try to formulate certain mental images as reminders. Such techniques as *ko tsuri goshi* and *tsuri komi goshi* sound similar and can be easily mistaken for each other. The simplest way to memorise these is to be able to translate, and the glossary of terms contains the majority of translations for the Japanese terms used in this book, as well as many others for general use.

Presuming that the student is now well versed in the syllabus, the next important stage of preparation concerns the *judogi*, which *must* be freshly laundered and well pressed. The student with a badly creased or dirty suit will stand out like a sore thumb, giving a bad impression to the grader. I have known an occasion when a student's suit was so dirty that he was turned away even before the start of the grading. A creased suit will not lose you marks but will have a detrimental effect if you are a borderline case.

Finally, of course, the student must be personally clean with short hair (or hair suitably tied back), clean and short fingernails and toenails, and clean hands and feet. Although this is part of the general rule applying to your *dojo*, it is surprising how many seem to forget these basics when going for grading.

Whilst awaiting your grading (one always seems to have a long wait), it is advisable not to eat anything. Grading on a full stomach will lead to indigestion and in some cases make you physically sick. I have seen students rushing to an open window a short time after commencing their grading through having eaten just before going on. Similarly, it is good sense to visit the cloakroom before the start as there is often no chance to go once the grading is under way.

All these tips are pure common sense to most people. However it is surprising how many will ignore them and they wondor why thcy had problems in their grading.

CONDUCT DURING GRADING

When you are being graded you are *not* in competition with your partner. It is not a case of one will pass and the other fail. The grader is not comparing the two of you, although this will be the case if one is obviously less experienced than the other.

The first thing to remember is that you *rei* to your grader at the start and finish of the grading. He or she will expect you to exercise or warm up for a few minutes prior to bowing you in to start. This warm-up should be confined to stretching exercises rather than power exercises. Your strength should be conserved at this point for later in the session.

Once you are into the grading you must *not* converse with your partner. You are permitted to indicate to your partner if you wish him or her to move in one way or the other or to change positions. You may talk to the grader but not unnecessarily. You may ask to do any throw again or in a different fashion, and your grader will set out the ground rules as regards that sort of thing; but if he or she does not, then do not try to exceed the advice I have given.

If you feel ill during a grading, do not continue until you are sick on the mat. Tell the grader and you will be allowed to sit down in the fresh air for a few minutes. If you feel that you cannot continue, you will then be excused and another Uke substituted in your place. This will mean that you will probably fail, unless the grading is almost over and you have demonstrated competence during the session. Sometimes you may be permitted to complete the grading at your own club, depending upon circumstances and the decision of the Master of Zen Judo.

If you are injured during a grading and cannot continue, the outcome again depends upon how you have done up to that point. You may be allowed to take the rest of the grading in your own club or you may be given the grade in some circumstances. If the grading is less than two-thirds complete you will probably have to take it again next time. Any decision is subject to the agreement of the Master.

The final result of your grading, in every case, is up to the Master or the Sensei in charge of the grading day. He or she usually takes heed of a grader's decision but may intervene if he or she feels that a student has been unjustly treated. As I have stated before, I have failed a grading at brown belt stage (probably through inexperience), but I did not let that failure deter me. If anything it made me all the more determined to pass next time.

The final part of the grading involves *shiai* (contest), and this is usually conducted personally by the Master or the Sensei in charge. If you have failed you will have been told so by this time and dismissed from the grading hall. Students over 40 years old are not expected to take part in *shiai*. This is purely a test of your determination to 'have a go', rather than of your competitive skill. Winning or losing is not important to the outcome of the grading; the Sensei is looking for fighting spirit. Groundwork does not feature very highly in this contest and prolonged grappling for a hold will normally be terminated in favour of standing techniques.

CONDUCTING A GRADING

Brown belts are expected to be able to grade up to orange belt within their own club. This is where the techniques of grading are learned under the guidance of the chief instructor. I do not intend to tell you how to conduct a grading — everyone has his or her particular ideas on this — so I shall confine myself to explaining the rationale behind the way I approach the task and leave it to the individual to adopt or adapt this as they will.

The first thing to remember is that the students are likely to be very nervous, so any show of indecision on your part will not add to their confidence. I always try to put the students at ease by sitting down with them and finding out their names, which club they are from and any other relevant facts such as how long they have been doing Judo, how often they practise, and so on. I explain that my job is to try to help them pass up to the next grade and that I won't fail them if they make any silly mistakes. We can all forget a couple of techniques in the heat of a grading, and I'm quite willing for them to return to one they've forgotten at the end of a section. I finish by explaining to them that all I'm doing is assessing whether they are ready and able to hold the next belt, and at the end of the day the marks they have gained are only figures on a piece of paper: it is the way they perform in both throwing and falling that counts.

Graders have many different ways of approaching the actual grading. Some will expect the students to repeat every throw several times just to ensure that they are quite exhausted at the finish. Others are happy with a single demonstration of a throw, marking the technique accordingly. I personally expect the student to perform each technique twice during the initial stages. The first time I look at the technique overall to get the feel of the way the student approaches it. On the repeat I look for detailed faults. On many occasions I would not require a repeat where the technique has been performed naturally and correctly.

The standard method of grading is to get the students to perform each technique to the right then each one to the left, changing the students around at the halfway stage so that both have performed and acted as Uke. One variation is where each student is asked to perform the technique directly after he or she has been thrown. Thus A throws B, B gets up and then throws A using the same technique, which saves changing them around at the halfway stage. This can be extended to include left-hand throws as well, when A throws B to the right, B gets up and throws A to the right, A gets up and throws B to the left and so on. These variations can work well when you are short of time and know that the students are thoroughly familiar with their techniques. They do not work so well with children, who have difficulty in following such a routine.

The rest of the grading is conducted in like manner, the combination techniques and counter techniques following on from the standing techniques. In certain cases a section of the grading may be purely demonstration, where the student must show the grader that he or she understands the technique or combination (for example, counter twos or two-by-twos). In such cases the number of techniques asked for is up to grader. When the grader feels that the student can show nothing more, the section is finished. This can take between ten and twenty techniques depending on how well the grader feels the students are doing.

When a student is obviously not up to the required standard, the grader must approach the grading carefully. Students who persistently forget throws or get them so wrong that they are unrecognisable, or who show no knowledge of a section of the syllabus, are obvious candidates for failure. The grader should try to give them every chance to improve their performance, and must not show anger or brusqueness. In such cases I have called a halt to gradings after the combination techniques section, mainly because the failing students have been holding up the grading for others. Where a grader has two students, of whom one is an obvious failure, the grading should continue to the end. In these cases I tend to accept whatever the failing student does without comment or criticism in order to speed up the grading in favour of the better student. It doesn't take long for the student who passes to realise what is happening.

At the completion of the grading, or where you have to dismiss a pair of students early, it is essential to explain to them why they have failed. Point out all the obvious faults and errors so that these may be practised before the next grading session. With children there is very often a flood of tears, which I personally find difficult to deal with. In such cases I usually seek out the parents, if they are around, or the children's chief instructor, and explain why they failed. A failure without explanation can lead to misunderstanding and bad feeling within the Zen Family.

TEACHING GRADES

A system of teaching grades has been introduced into the Zen Family which may apply to certain players. Where players suffer an accident or chronic illness which renders them unable to fully participate on the mat, teaching grades may be considered. In cases of strains or sprains the player will be back to full health within a relatively short time. In other cases, such as severe dislocations or broken bones or chronic illness, the player may be unable to practise for many months. It was felt that provision should be made for those showing dedication in the form of teaching lower belts by the award of 'teaching' grades. This system is designed to accommodate those who are satisfied to continue on the basis of limited participation.

It is essential to realise that this system is not designed as an alternative or easier method of achieving grades. It is a system offering encouragement to those who may well otherwise quit Judo following lengthy illness or injuries.

Teaching grades relate only to green belts and above. The candidate must have been teaching lower belts for some time previously and should have qualified in the normal manner for green belt. To qualify for the next grade the student will need to be competent to teach the syllabus for that belt. This competence must be amply demonstrated to the examiner. In addition, the student should be capable of performing the majority of the full syllabus (within the constraints of the disability) to a degree which would satisfy the examiner at a normal grading. Where certain techniques cannot be performed, these will be recorded on the grading sheet for future reference.

To attain a teaching grade the candidate need not be used as Uke, nor will he or she be required to perform *randori* or *shiai* unless able to do so. The grading may be stretched over several sessions and performed at the candidate's own club with the Master's permission. The grading, however, must be performed by a 3rd Dan or above.

This system operates up to 2nd Dan only; thereafter any subsequent Dan grades will be awarded at the discretion of the Master of Zen Judo in whatever manner he decides. These may continue to be teaching grades or may be full grades according to circumstances prevailing at the time.

Conversion to full grade is available to any teaching grade if wished. A conversion grading will take the form of the candidate performing all techniques and moves that were omitted at the last teaching grading, and acting as Uke for a grading at that level. Any conversion will be performed at the headquarters *dojo* with the Master's permission.

Licences or membership cards are endorsed with the suffix 'T' against the grade to indicate when a teaching grade is held. After conversion the appropriate grade box is dated and signed by the examiner.

GRADES IN ZEN JUDO

In many other styles of Judo different grades are utilised for junior members. This is a useful system where gradings are based upon competition. In the Zen Family all candidates, adults and children, either sex, are expected to perform the same grading examinations. The standards marked are similar throughout. Therefore there is no distinction between junior and senior grades.

The only stipulation on age is that juniors are generally not allowed to grade for their black belts until the age of 14. This, however, is subject to any exception that the Master of Zen Judo may permit. In certain exceptional cases where a student shows particular promise and has the correct attitude, an early black belt grading has been allowed.

The Zen Judo Family grading system is as follows:

Juniors/Adults

Novice	white belt
Gokyu (5th Kyu)	yellow belt
Yonkyu (4th Kyu)	orange belt
Sankyu (3rd Kyu)	green belt
Nikyu (2nd Kyu)	blue belt
Ikkyu (1st Kyu)	brown belt

Adults (over 14)

Shodan (1st Dan)	black belt
Nidan (2nd Dan)	black Belt
Sandan (3rd Dan)	black belt
Yondan (4th Dan)	black Belt
Godan (5th Dan)	black Belt
Rokudan (6th Dan)	red/white blocked belt
Shichidan (7th Dan)	red/white
Hachidan (8th Dan)	red/white
Kudan (9th Dan)	red belt
Judan (10th Dan)	red belt

Black belts from 1st to 5th Dan are differentiated by the appropriate number of Dan grade rings which they wear at the bottom of their belts.

9
ATEMIWAZA

Atemiwaza is the art of attacking vital spots, and is rarely included within the instruction given to Kyu grades. Because of the intrinsic dangers associated with *atemiwaza*, it is a subject only touched upon in this manual. Close instruction in this subject is only imparted to Dan grades, who should have developed both the physical skills and the moral qualities to be able to use this knowledge without abuse.

In our modern society, however, the growing popularity of other martial arts which utilise *atemi*, such as Karate, Kempo, Kung Fu or Tae Kwon Do, has brought the hitherto secret techniques of *atemiwaza* out into the open. It is with this in mind that I feel obliged to include some basic *atemiwaza* in this text.

I always make a point of coaching my Dan grade students not only in the throwing and grappling techniques of Judo, but also to be able to finish their technique using *atemi* so that their aggressor will be unlikely to give them further trouble for a while. Such coaching forms a very minor part of the training, however, and occurs only occasionally.

To be able to strike an opponent correctly with your fist requires previous coaching in boxing, Karate or other martial arts. Women members of the club will usually be rather weak at this and it is better for them to learn to strike with elbow or foot. In this chapter I shall concentrate on the methods of striking where your opponent has been thrown and is lying on the ground, momentarily dazed. This is the time when your aggressor becomes vulnerable, just after you have managed to throw him or her, and it is usually for only a couple of seconds after he or she has hit the ground. It is at this moment that the finishing *atemi* may be successfully applied. Once your aggressor has realised where he or she is, and where you are, he or she becomes prepared for further attack and your blows are expected.

STRIKING POINTS

The body possesses many parts with which you may strike an opponent; not just the front of the knuckles as is popularly supposed. In any study of *atemi* a thorough knowledge of these parts is necessary for the student to be prepared.

Fist

The forefist is the most widely used attacking tool in the martial arts. One point to bear in mind, though, is that a strong blow to a bony part of your opponent's body will impart equal pain to your fist unless you are well practised in the art of punching. The back of the knuckles of the fore and middle fingers is quite strong and may be employed for attacking the head area.

Atemi by fist can follow a successful throw. Here Tori has just thrown Uke and has followed down on to one knee with a fist blow at the same time.

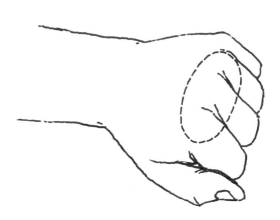

Striking points – the fist

Elbow

There are three parts of the elbow which may be utilised in a close fighting situation: the front, the tip and the back of the elbow. The tip is the most useful in the situations described here.

An elbow strike can be very effective if directed to the vital parts of Uke's body. Here Tori utilises his elbow to Uke's crotch to temporarily disable his opponent.

Hand-Edge

The fleshy edge of the open hand on the little-finger side makes a useful weapon for certain strikes, for instance to windpipe, temples or nose.

Fingers

Straight finger strikes are not normally advised unless you are well practised. They can be utilised, however, to the eyes or testicles of an aggressor with great effect for little expenditure of energy.

Feet

The ball of the foot, with toes turned upwards, makes an effective kicking weapon. Again this requires much practice, and a better all-round weapon is the heel (especially if covered by a heavy shoe). The side of the foot also provides a good, strong kicking weapon.

From a standing position the foot makes a useful weapon following a throw. Care must be taken to ensure that its use is effective. Here Tori stamps to the face or neck to finish his opponent.

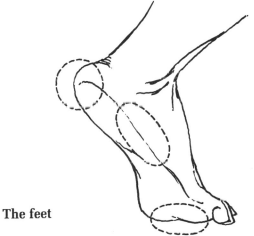

The feet

Knee

The kneecap is strong and solid once the knee is tightly bent, and may be used to effect during close fighting.

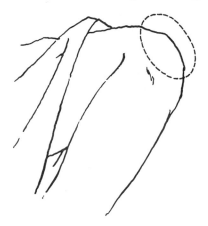

Head

Attacks with the forehead should only be utilised in extremely close situations. A head butt which goes wrong will leave you in a very vulnerable position.

VITAL SPOTS

The body contains many vital spots and only a few of the more widely known ones are discussed here. Many of the spots must be attacked with great precision to achieve success, and are therefore of little use in a self-defence situation. The spots which I would try to attack in a situation which calls for aggressive defence are shown below:

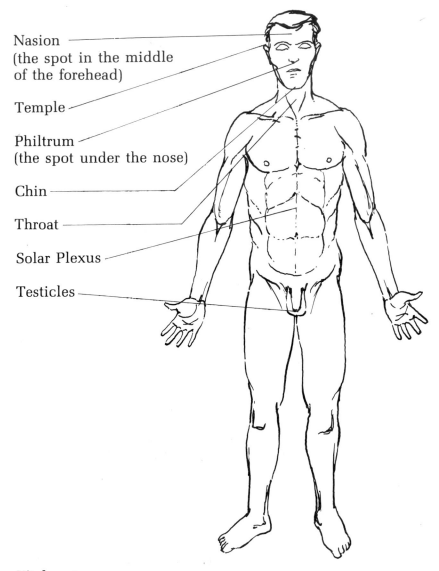

Nasion
(the spot in the middle
of the forehead)

Temple

Philtrum
(the spot under the nose)

Chin

Throat

Solar Plexus

Testicles

Vital spots

Nasion

The spot in the middle of the forehead which may be hit by fist or hand-edge. A blow to this spot renders your opponent in great pain and unable to co-ordinate for a short space of time, sufficient for you to make your escape.

Temple

If struck with fist or hand-edge on the temples, the receiver will be rendered unconscious for a short time.

Philtrum

The spot directly under the nose, which may be struck by fist, hand-edge or elbow. It is very sensitive and a blow to this area renders the victim helpless for a short time.

Chin

May be attacked by fist or elbow to render the victim unconscious for some time.

Throat

The front of the throat/windpipe is a very vulnerable spot. An open-hand blow across this area will constrict the windpipe, which may have lethal consequences. This should only be used in a life-threatening situation.

Solar Plexus

This spot may be attacked using fist, elbow, knee or foot. One of the most vulnerable spots in the human body.

Testicles

May be attacked using fist, straight fingers, elbow, knee or foot. Even a light blow to this area is sufficient to render your opponent harmless for a while. Accuracy is not vital as a near miss can do almost as much damage.

This list of seven spots is by no means exhaustive, and many others are known to practitioners of the martial arts. Certain of the arts specialise in rendering their partners unconscious, by attacking vital parts which I have not mentioned here, and then practising revival techniques on them.

FINISHING TECHNIQUES

Players who wish to practise finishing techniques should only do so with the knowledge and consent of their partners. Punches or other blows should not connect with the vital spots aimed for, but should stop a few centimetres from contact. The fist, hand, elbow or foot should pull back once the blow has been delivered.

With all throwing techniques, the easiest entry for *atemi* is to perform a half-sacrifice technique, landing on your right knee. Your right fist will be drawn back as you touch the ground and the blow is made straight from the side, as with the *oi zuki* punch in Karate. You must pull back immediately, ready to strike again should your first blow not have connected correctly. Alternatively, the elbow strike to the solar plexus must draw back in readiness to follow up.

When you do not go down into a half-sacrifice, the right foot may be utilised for a finishing *atemi* to the face, solar plexus or testicles. You must remember that a blow with the foot is usually much heavier than one with the hand (unless you are an expert in other martial arts), and care must be taken not to badly injure an attacker or you may find that you yourself are in trouble.

IN CONCLUSION

There is little doubt that the very fact that your attacker is thrown on the street may be sufficient to deter him or her, or even cause enough damage to prevent the attacker continuing his or her attack. The added *atemi* will probably ensure that you can make your escape easily. Where there is more than one assailant, the throw and *atemi* should ensure that you can concentrate upon the other attacker(s) without worrying what the first assailant is about. Usually a second attacker is somewhat loath to press the attack having witnessed the disabling of his or her partner. One must bear in mind that it is usually the stronger and more confident of two attackers who will make the first move, and if you can disable him or her the other will be at a psychological disadvantage.

Judo is a training for life. Not only does it generate self-confidence, it also helps with elements of self-control such as patience, even temper, and understanding others. The application of Zen may be illustrated by describing an encounter which I had when I was a senior Kyu grade. I was suddenly confronted by a gentleman of impressive stature, several inches taller than myself and somewhat broader, who expressed a desire to give me a 'bunch of fives'. This was a situation which had suddenly blown up in my professional capacity as a health officer, the details of which I shall spare you. To say the least, I was quite taken aback when I found myself in this eyeball-to-eyeball encounter. My reply came absolutely automatically, and if I had stopped to think I wouldn't have said, 'You aren't bloody big enough.' I was just beginning to feel the first pangs of incontinence. But his reaction was to step back and pause for thought. Then he said, 'You're an expert at Judo, aren't you?' My reply was, 'I wouldn't call myself that.' That marked the termination of the encounter, fairly mundane in nature and nothing that many would find out of the ordinary in their daily lives. What marks it as different was the fact that my reaction came automatically and quite out of character. The de-escalation of the situation which followed is very much in the spirit of the Zen Judo Family, and one must never test one's skills by picking a fight.

The spirit of Zen Judo can be said to be the art of 'fighting without fighting' (to borrow a quotation from Bruce Lee in his film *Enter the Dragon*), and Sensei McCarthy has always stressed the peaceful settlement of any interpersonal dispute. The points mentioned in this chapter on *atemi* will be of no use when a peaceful settlement is indicated. They may, however, give you the means to a quicker settlement if peace is not in the mind of your antagonist.

10
THE SPIRIT OF ZEN

This book is deeply concerned with the techniques associated with Zen Judo, and has been slanted towards the grading syllabus for Kyu grades up to 1st Dan. The gradings thereafter mainly concern the acquisition of skills in *kata* and precision in techniques taught previously. The syllabus to 4th Dan, the *katas* and the extension of groundwork in the areas of locks and strangles, will be the subject for a further book at a later date. The question that may well be asked now is, where is all this leading?

As I have stated before, Zen Judo is not competition oriented, and thus the skills in groundwork are neglected to the benefit of standing techniques. This is one area where other styles of Judo usually excel and the Zen player may be at a distinct disadvantage. Be this as it may, the popularity of Zen Judo with many of its devotees is partly due to this lack of grappling on the mat and the cleanliness of its techniques, and I would be the last to suggest that more *newaza* is introduced. Groundwork may be important in winning competitions, but Zen Judo is not directed at this goal and thus should follow a different path.

The question has arisen as to exactly where Zen Judo *is* directed. Not having extracted a precise answer from Sensei McCarthy on this point, I shall give my own thoughts for what they are worth. Primarily, I see Zen Judo as a martial art rather than a competitive sport. I see Zen standing apart from the other styles and associations in its objectives and in its accent upon technique. This view has been supported by Dan grades from all other associations who have visited me, the majority advising me that we have a unique style and outlook which is both refreshing and more akin to the original concept of Judo. At the end of the day a true martial art must obey the Japanese code of *bushido* (the moral ethical code of the Samurai leaders) and the principles of *jita kyoyei* (individual advancement benefits society as a whole).

The development of Zen Judo along these lines is still in its early stages and requires more positive guidance from the top. I feel that only now am I able to perceive the fine dividing line between a sport and a martial art. I am working on the development of my Judo in many areas, and I will briefly outline these. I would stress that these are my personal feelings and do not necessarily reflect those of other Zen players of an equal or higher status than I.

USE OF *KI*

Many people, including Judoka, will begin to scoff at even the mention of *ki* (a psychic energy said to be centred in the lower abdomen). However, the true masters in all martial arts are well aware of its existence and many are able to demonstrate it. Many of the feats of the Karate, Aikido and Judo masters cannot be accounted for except by explanations involving *ki*.

The ideal throw is accomplished without the utilisation of strength on the part of Tori. All you need do is blend with the movement of Uke and apply the technique. Correct breathing (*kokyu*) and concentration of *ki* will be sufficient to enable the technique to be completed without any excess muscular involvement. This happens to almost everyone occasionally during *randori*, and one is left with the question afterwards: 'What did I do?' or 'How did I do that?'

The development of control over one's *ki* is a long and difficult road to travel, many falling by the wayside. I do not know whether I shall meet with even partial success in this direction, but I am taking the first steps towards this goal through the study of Aikido.

TAKING THE MIND

Simple techniques may be successfully utilised when the player manages to direct the mind or concentration of Uke away from the intended technique. A simple illustration of this is the way that the expert Badminton player will look one way and play the shot to a totally different place. Your eyes, and consequently your focus, are drawn to the spot where your opponent is looking. If your opponent appears to be effecting a technique to a certain direction, even your balance will be affected. When the throw is executed, you may well be caught completely off balance or 'out of focus', and the throw will take you by surprise.

Although not closely related to the use of *ki*, this technique can be allied to it to produce devastating effects from a simple throw such as *ashi gake*.

Again, my development along these lines is still in its infancy but promises to become a useful adjunct to my performance one day.

FINISHING TECHNIQUE

In the chapter on *atemi* I stressed the importance of the use of a finish to your throws. Development along these lines is still progressing, and the various forms of *atemi* are being tried out carefully for effectiveness and control. Tuition in this has not proved easy, and must follow only when the student is naturally falling into the correct posture at the termination of the throw. To date, such instruction has been confined to blue belts and above, and they are warned only to use such methods in a last-resort situation. The use of *atemi* as an alternative means of taking the mind is currently being tried, and appears to be an effective adjunct to some throws at the point of entry.

As you will appreciate, there is considerable work to be put into the development of Zen Judo for it to reach the point where I am satisfied that the criteria of a martial art are met. Some have pointed out that this is combining Judo with elements of Karate, Aikido and Ju Jitsu, and the end product will be neither one thing nor another, a viewpoint to which they are indeed entitled and which I would not endeavour to change. Judo and Aikido were, after all, developed from the original forms of Ju Jitsu and some reversion would not go amiss. One must also note that both Karate and Aikido contain moves within their syllabus which can be classed as Judo, so there is no shame in the converse.

My personal viewpoint is that if Zen Judo is not to become a competitive sport (a move that I would abhor), then it must be developed as an effective martial art which has practical use in a dangerous situation, and it is to this goal that I would foresee its development. By saying this I do not imply any criticism of other Judo styles, as they have been proven to be effective in such situations.

Change is not always a good thing, and I would not wish to depart from the syllabus; rather, I would see it extended in the directions mentioned. All students who are taught by me are well aware of my feelings on this subject, and most appear receptive to my aims. I can only hope that in the years to come they will also attempt further development along the lines that I have summarised.

My message to whoever decides to continue in my direction is not to take heed of the many who only have a mind for basic Judo. Extend your horizons by the study of other martial arts and learn from them. Any martial art studied in isolation is sterile. Its practitioners will never develop beyond a certain level and will never experience the wonder of continuing to learn new technique, or new variations on established technique, and feeling the change within themselves with the accumulation of knowledge.

The title of this book indicates that, to me, Zen Judo is not just another sport or pastime: it has become my way of life. To really appreciate and understand any martial art it must permeate your being and become reflected in everything you do. Words are not sufficient to describe the ways that this can happen, you will one day simply come to realise that this has occurred and your only path forward lies within the ways of *bushido*.

This is how I would describe the spirit of Zen Judo, and I sincerely hope that one day you too will fully understand and recognise what it is that I am talking about. This book only describes technique; the rest lies with you.

I end with a quotation from Kyuzo Mifune, 10th Dan, who said:

One does not acquire powerful friends without making strong enemies, as a man acquires substance, so he arouses the covetousness of those who would tear him down, like jackals, and devour him – that he be afflicted, in addition, with the immature antics of associates, who appear as grown men, but are in fact as irresponsible and heedless as children would seem to ensure his destruction.

APPENDIX A –
THE FULL SYLLABUS

WHITE TO YELLOW SYLLABUS

The full syllabus for grading to 5th Kyu is as follows:

Ukemiwaza (breakfalls)
  Mae korobi – forward rolling breakfall
  Ushiro ukemi – rear breakfall
  Migi yoko ukemi – right side breakfall
  Hidari yoko ukemi – left side breakfall
  Mae ukemi – front breakfall

Tachiwaza (standing techniques)

All throws to be performed to the right and to the left.
  Kubi nage – neck throw
  Ashi gake – ankle block
  Ko uchi maki komi – minor inner winding
  Tai otoshi – body drop

Osaekomiwaza (hold-down techniques)

  Hon kesa gatame – scarf hold
  Kazure kesa gatame – broken scarf hold

Renzokuwaza (combination throws)

A technique two to each standing technique to the right.

Kaeshiwaza (counter throws)

A counter one to each standing technique to the right.

Randori (free practice)

Students will show the standing techniques, combination techniques and counters on the move.

YELLOW TO ORANGE SYLLABUS

The full syllabus for grading to 4th Kyu is as follows:

Ukemiwaza (breakfalls)

The same falls as in the previous syllabus, although students will be expected to perform much better than in the previous grading.

Tachiwaza (standing techniques)

All throws to be performed to the right and to the left.
  Kubi nage
  Ashi gake
  Ko uchi maki komi
  Tai otoshi
  Kata seoi – shoulder carry
  Ryo ashi dori – two-hands ankle hold
  Hiza guruma – knee wheel
  Uki goshi – floating hip
  Obi goshi – belt hip
  Eri nage – lapel throw
  O soto guruma – major wheel
  To hiza sasae – hand knee prop
NB Two versions of *o soto guruma* will be required.
Short and long versions of *te hiza sasae* are required.

Osaekomiwaza (hold-down techniques)

  Hon kesa gatame
  Kazure kesa gatame
  Kata gatame – shoulder hold
  Makura kesa gatame – pillow cross-chest hold

Renzokuwaza (San) (combination throws)

A technique three to each standing technique will be performed to the right and to the left.

Kaeshiwaza (Ich) (counter throws)

A counter one to each standing technique will be performed to the right and to the left.

Kaeshiwaza (Ni) (counter combinations)

A counter two to each standing technique will be performed to the right side only.

Nage-Osaekomiwaza (throws to groundhold)
Demonstration of throws to groundholds will be performed to the right side only.

Randori

Shiai (contest)

ORANGE TO GREEN SYLLABUS

The syllabus for grading to 3rd Kyu is as follows:

Ukemiwaza (breakfalls)

Mae korobi to migi and hidari – rolling breakfall to the right and left sides.
Other breakfalls as in the previous gradings.

Tachiwaza (standing techniques)

All throws to be performed to the right and to the left.
Kubi nage
Ashi gake
Ko uchi maki komi
Tai otoshi
Kata seoi
Ryo ashi dori
Hiza guruma
Uki goshi
Obi goshi
Eri nage
O soto guruma
Te hiza sasae
Kata nage – shoulder throw
Ashi guruma – leg wheel
(Morote) seoi nage – both arms shoulder throw
Sasae tsuri komi ashi – propping lifting ankle block
O guruma – major wheel
Ko soto gake – small outer hook
Ko tsuri goshi – minor hip throw
Koshi guruma – hip wheel

Osaekomiwaza (hold-down techniques)

Hon kesa gatame
Kazure kesa gatame
Kata gatame
Makura kesa gatame
Ushiro kesa gatame – rear cross-chest hold
Mune gatame – chest hold

Hoan Sutemiwaza (half-sacrifice techniques)

Half-sacrifices to be performed to the right and to the left.
Kubi nage
Ashi gake
Tai otoshi
Kata seoi

Renzokuwaza (San) (combination throws)

A technique three to each standing technique to the right and the left.

Kaeshiwaza (Ich) (counter throws)

A counter one to each standing technique will be performed to the right and to the left.

Kaeshiwaza (Ni) (counter combinations)

A counter two to each standing technique will be performed to the right and to the left.

Kaeshiwaza (Ni X Ni) (counter two-by-twos)

Counter two-by-twos to be demonstrated to the right and to the left.

Nage-Osaekomiwaza (throws to groundhold)

Demonstration of throws to groundholds will be performed to right and left sides.

Randori

Shiai

GREEN TO BLUE SYLLABUS

The full syllabus for grading to 2nd Kyu is as follows:

Ukemiwaza (breakfalls)

This is the same syllabus as was performed for your previous grading.

Tachiwaza (standing techniques)

All techniques as for the previous gradings, plus the following to be performed to the left and to the right:
O soto otoshi – major outer drop
Tsuri komi goshi – lift-pull hip
Sode tsuri komi goshi – sleeve lift-pull hip
Uchi ashi gake – inner leg block
Ko soto gari – small outer reap
Hiki tai – sleeve pull
Uchi ashi sasae – inner leg prop
Kata ashi dori – advancing side leg

Osaekomiwaza (hold-down techniques)

Groundholds from all previous gradings plus the following further two holds:
Hon yoko shiho gatame – side locking four-quarters hold
Kazure yoko shiho gatame – broken side locking four-quarters hold

Han Sutemiwaza (half-sacrifice techniques)

Half-sacrifices to be performed to the left and to the right.
Kubi nage
Ashi gake
Tai otoshi
Kata seoi
Uki goshi
Kata nage

Renzokuwaza (Yon) (combination throws)

A technique four to each standing technique to right and left sides.

Kaeshiwaza (Ich) (counter throws)

A counter one to each standing technique will be performed to the right and to the left.

Kaeshiwaza (Ni) (counter combinations)

A counter two to each standing technique will be performed to the right and to the left.

Kaeshiwaza (Ni X Ni) (counter two-by-twos)

Counter two-by-twos to be demonstrated to the right and to the left.

Nage-Osaekomiwaza (throws to groundhold)

Demonstration of throws to groundholds will be performed to right and left sides.

Sutemiwaza (sacrifice techniques)

The following full sacrifices to be performed to the right and left sides:
Yoko wakare – side separation
Uki waza – floating throw
Sumi gaeshi – corner counter

Kaeshi Sutemi (counter sacrifices)

Demonstration of sacrifice counters to both right- and left-hand throws.

Randori

Shiai

BLUE TO BROWN SYLLABUS

The full syllabus for grading to 1st Kyu is as follows:

Ukemiwaza (breakfalls)

This is the same syllabus as was performed for your previous grading.

Tachiwaza (standing techniques)

All techniques as for the previous gradings, plus the following to be performed to the left and to the right:
Soto gake – outer hook
Harai tsuri komi ashi – lift-pull foot sweep
O soto gari – major outer reaping throw
Sumi otoshi – corner drop
Hiji otoshi – elbow drop
Hane goshi – spring hip
Kata guruma – shoulder wheel

Osaekomiwaza (hold-down techniques)

Groundholds from all previous gradings plus the following two further holds, to be performed to the right and to the left:
Kazure kami shiho gatame – broken upper four-quarters hold
Hon tate shiho gatame – straight locking four-quarters hold

Han Sutemiwaza (half-sacrifice techniques)

Half-sacrifices to be performed to the right and to the left:
Kubi nage
Ashi gake
Tai otoshi
Kata seoi
Uki goshi
Kata nage
(Morote) seoi nage
Hiki tai

Renzokuwaza (Yon) (combination throws)

A technique four to each standing technique to right and left sides.

Kaeshiwaza (Ich) (counter throws)

A counter one to each standing technique will be performed to the right and to the left.

Kaeshiwaza (Ni) (counter combinations)

A counter two to each standing technique will be performed to the right and to the left.

Kaeshiwaza (Ni X Ni) (counter two-by-twos)

Counter two-by-twos to be demonstrated to the right and to the left.

Nage-Osaekomiwaza (throws to groundhold)

Demonstration of throws to groundholds will be performed to right and left sides.

Sutemiwaza (sacrifice techniques)

The following full sacrifice techniques will be performed to right and left sides:
Yoko wakare
Uki waza
Sumi gaeshi
Tomoe nage – circular throw
Yoko guruma – side wheel
Tani otoshi – valley drop
Towara gaeshi – rice bale throw

Kaeshi Sutemi (counter sacrifices)

Demonstration of sacrifice counters to both right and left side throws.

Han Sutemiwaza (Ni) (half-sacrifice twos)

Demonstration of half-sacrifice twos to both right and left sides.

Sutemiwaza (Ni) (sacrifice twos)

Demonstration of sacrifice twos to right and left sides.

Randori

Shiai

BROWN TO BLACK SYLLABUS

The full syllabus for grading to 1st Dan is as follows:

Ukemiwaza (breakfalls)

This is the same syllabus as was performed for your previous grading.

Tachiwaza (standing techniques)

All techniques as for the previous gradings, plus the following to be performed to the left and to the right:

Okuri ashi barai – following foot sweep
O uchi gari – major inner reaping throw
Uchi mata – inner thigh throw
De ashi barai – advanced foot sweep
Harai goshi – sweeping loin throw
Ko uchi gari – minor inner reaping throw
O goshi – major hip throw

Osaekomiwaza (hold-down techniques)

Groundholds from all previous gradings plus the following two further holds, to be performed to the right and to the left:

Hon kami shiho gatame – Upper four-quarters hold
Kazure tate shiho gatame – Broken straight locking four-quarters Hold

Han Sutemiwaza (half-sacrifice techniques)

Half-sacrifices to be performed to the right and to the left:

Kubi nage
Ashi gake
Tai otoshi
Kata seoi
Uki goshi
Kata nage
(Morote) seoi nage
Hiki tai
Obi goshi
Eri nage
Te hiza sasae
Ko tsuri goshi
Koshi guruma
Tsuri komi goshi

Renzokuwaza (Go) (combination throws)

A technique five of each standing technique to right and left sides.

Kaeshiwaza (Ich) (counter throws)

A counter one to each standing technique will be performed to the right and to the left.

Kaeshiwaza (Ni) (counter combinations)

A counter two to each standing technique will be performed to the right and to the left.

Kaeshiwaza (Ni X Ni) (counter two-by-twos)

Counter two-by-twos to be demonstrated to the right and to the left.

Nage-Osaekomiwaza (throws to groundhold)

Demonstration of throws to groundholds will be performed to right and left sides.

Sutemiwaza (sacrifice techniques)

The following full sacrifice techniques will be performed to the right and left sides:

Yoko wakare
Uki waza
Sumi gaeshi
Tomoe nage
Yoko guruma
Tani otoshi
Tawara gaeshi
Yoko gake – side block
Yoko otoshi – side drop
Ura nage – back throw
Korobi sutemi – rolling sacrifice
Soto maki komi – outer wraparound throw
Hane maki komi – springing wraparound throw

Kaeshi Sutemi (counter sacrifices)

Demonstration of sacrifice counters to both right and left side throws.

Han Sutemiwaza (San) (half-sacrifice threes)

Demonstration of half-sacrifice threes to both right and left sides.

Sutemiwaza (San) (sacrifice threes)

Demonstration of sacrifice threes to right and left sides.

Kagamiwaza (mirror technique – solo fighting)

Demonstrations as both Tori and Uke to be performed to right and left sides.

Randori

Shiai

APPENDIX B –
FORMS FOR USE IN GRADINGS

THE ZEN JUDO FAMILY

REGISTRATION FORM

Name of Judo Player ....

Date of Birth ....

Parent/Guardian (if under 18) ....

Address ....

....

....

Telephone Number   Home   ....

                     Work   ....

Previous Injuries (Please note any major injuries received prior to filling in this form.)

....

....

A. To Be Signed by Parent/Guardian if Player is Under 18

As the parent/guardian of the above named player, I understand that the techniques taught in Judo can be extremely dangerous if practised off the mat. I will therefore do my best to ensure that the above named player will not use Judo off the mat except in a life-threatening situation.

In the full knowledge that Judo is a sport in which injury may occur, I hold the Zen Judo Family officials, leaders, instructors, referees and assistants harmless from all claims of any kind resulting from injury, damages or losses, howsoever arising.

Signed ....

Date   ....

B. To Be Signed by a Player Over 18

I wish to partake in the activities of the Zen Judo Family in the full knowledge that Judo is a sport in which injury may occur. In doing so I hold the Family's officials, leaders, instructors, referees and assistants harmless from all claims of any kind resulting from injury, damages or losses, howsoever arising.

Signed ....

Date   ....

GRADING RECORD

Grade	Date	Comments
Yellow	. . . .	. . . .
Orange	. . . .	. . . .
Green	. . . .	. . . .
Blue	. . . .	. . . .
Brown	. . . .	. . . .
Black	. . . .	. . . .
	. . . .	. . . .
	. . . .	. . . .

ZEN JUDO FAMILY GRADING FORM – WHITE TO YELLOW
THE ZEN JUDO FAMILY

	UKEMI	STANDING TECHNIQUES				LEFT-HAND TECHNIQUES			
		KUBI NAGE	ASHI GAKE	KO UCHI MAKI KOMI	TAI OTOSHI	KUBI NAGE	ASHI GAKE	KO UCHI MAKI KOMI	TAI OTOSHI
MAXIMUM MARK POSSIBLE	10	5	5	5	5	2	2	2	2

...CHNIQUE ...OS			COUNTERS				GROUND-HOLDS			
ASHI GAKE	KO UCHI MAKI KOMI	TAI OTOSHI	KUBI NAGE	ASHI GAKE	KO UCHI MAKI KOMI	TAI OTOSHI	1	2	RANDORI	TOTAL
3	3	3	3	3	3	3	3	3	10	78

DATE _____

CLUB _____

EXAMINER'S NAME _____

SIGNATURE _____

THE ZEN JUDO FAMILY

121

CLUB ....

DATE OF GRADING ....

	GUIDES	MAXIMUM MARKS	
	D	10	UKEMI
	*	40	TECH. 1 MIGI
	*	20	TECH. 1 HIDARI
	*	20	TECHNIQUE 3 R/L
	*	20	KAESHI 1 R/L
	D	10	KAESHI 2
	D	10	THROWS TO HOLD
	D	10	4 GROUNDHOLDS
		20	RANDORI
		10	SHIAI
		170	TOTAL
		(119)	OUTCOME

D – Demonstration
* – To Each Named Technique

TECHNIQUE LIST
KUBI NAGE
ASHI GAKE
KO UCHI MAKI KOMI
TAI OTOSHI
KATA SEOI
RYO ASHI DORI
HIZA GURUMA
UKI GOSHI
OBI GOSHI
ERI NAGE
O SOTO GURUMA
TE HIZA SASAE

Pass Mark is 70% (119)

EXAMINER'S NAME (Printed)

EXAMINER'S SIGNATURE

122

GLOSSARY OF TERMS

Arashi Storm.
Ashi Leg or foot.
Atemiwaza Hitting and punching techniques.
Ayumi Ashi A manner of walking in which each foot leads the other successively.

Barai To sweep or sweeping.
Bokken Curved wooden practice sword.
Bushi A leader of the Samurai.
Bushido The moral ethical code of the *bushi*.

Chikar Power – to use one's strength.
Chitsai Small.

Dan Black belt rank.
De Advance
Deshi Student or pupil.
Do The way, the truth, the path.
Dojo Practice hall or place of enlightenment.
Dori Grasp or grab.
Dosa An exercise.
Dozo Please.

Eri Collar or lapel.

Fusegu To defend.

Gaeshi To counter (also *kueshi*).
Gake Hooking.
Garami To entangle, wrap or bend.
Gari Reaping
Gatame Lock or hold (also *katame*).
Gedan Lower area of the body.
Gi Training uniform.
Go Five.
Gonokata Forms of strength.
Goshi Hip (also *koshi*).
Goshin Jitsu The art of self-protection in all its forms.
Guruma Wheel.
Gyaku Reverse, opposite or alternative.
Gyaku Hanmi Opposite posture from opponent.

Ha Wing.
Hachi Eight.
Hadaka Naked or bare.
Hairikata Way of entering for a technique.
Hajime Start or begin.
Hakama Long shirt-like formal wear.
Hane Spring or jump.
Hanmi Triangular stance.
Hantai To oppose.

Hantei Decision required.
Hara Stomach or centre.
Harai Sweep.
Henke Blending.
Hidari Left (as opposed to right).
Hiji Elbow.
Hiki Pull.
Hiza Knee.
Ho Direction.
Hon Basic.

Ichi or *Ik* One.
Ippon Point or ten points.
Irimi Entering movement.

Jigotai Defensive posture.
Jime Strangle
Jita Kyoyei The principle that individual advancement benefits society as a whole.
Jitsu Art.
Jo Straight pole about four feet long.
Jodan Upper area of the body.
Joseki Place of honour in the *dojo* where teachers or important people sit.
Ju Gentle, or ten.
Judo Gentle way.
Judogi Judo clothing.
Judoka One who practises Judo.
Juji Cross.
Ju-Jitsu Gentle art.
Junokata The forms of gentleness, or showing the principles of giving way.
Jushin Centre of gravity.

Kaeshi To counter (also *Gaeshi*)
Kake The point of the throw or point of maximum power.
Kamae Stance.
Kami Upper or top.
Kamiza Upper seat, the instructors' side of the *dojo*.
Kansetsu Knuckle or joint.
Kata Form – a stylised set of techniques used to develop a performer's posture, balance and appreciation of the various Judo techniques, or one side or shoulder.
Katame Lock or hold (also *Gatame*).
Katame no kata The forms of grappling. Formal demonstrations of groundholds, strangle holds and joint-locking techniques.
Katsu Method of revival or artificial respiration for unconscious persons.

123

Kazure Broken or adapted.
Keiko Practice.
Ken Sword.
Kesa Scarf – actually a Bhuddist monk's surplice worn across the body.
Ki Psychic energy said to be centred in the lower abdomen, or the vital force of the body.
Kiai Summoning of spirit by shouting.
Kihon Basic form of a technique.
Kime To decide.
Kime no Kata Forms of decision – the *kata* of self-protection.
Kiri Cut, as with a knife.
Kiske Heels together.
Ko Small or minor.
Kodokan Institute of Judo in Japan.
Kokyu Breath – enery/*ki* flow.
Kokyu Ryoku The power harnessed through practising *kokyu*.
Korobi Rolling
Koshi Hip (also *Goshi*)
Kote Wrist.
Ku Nine.
Kubi Neck.
Kumikata Techniques of grasping the opponent.
Kuzushi Breaking of the opponent's balance.
Kwai Society or club.
Kyu Student grades.

Ma Exact or absolutely.
Ma ai Fighting distance (means harmony of space).
Machi-do jo Back-street gymnasium.
Mae Forwards.
Maki-Komi A compound word meaning to wind or winding.
Makura Pillow.
Manaka Centre.
Masutemiwaza Back sacrifice techniques.
Mata The inside top of the thigh.
Matte Wait or break.
Mawari To turn round.
Meijin Expert or master.
Men Face or head.
Mi Human body.
Migi Right (as opposed to left).
Mizu Water.
Mon Gate or junior grade in some styles of Judo.
Morote Both arms or hands.
Mune Chest.

Nage Throw.
Nage-no-Kata The forms of throwing. 15 selected throws executed to left and right to train the participants in body control and appreciation of Judo technique.
Name Wave (of water).
Nami To place in a line.
Ne To lie down.
Newaza Techniques done in a lying down position.
Ni Two
No Of.

O Major or big.
Obi Belt or sash.
Oi Centre or abdomen.
Oi Tsuki Thrust to centre.

Okii Big.
Okuri To send forwards.
Osaekomi Holding.
Oshi To push.
Otoshi To drop.
Owari End.
Oyo-Waza Variations of basic technique.

Randori Free practice.
Rei Bow.
Reigi Etiquette.
Rei wozuru Everybody will bow.
Reishiki Etiquette.
Renrakuwaza Combination techniques (also *renzokuwaza*).
Renzokuwaza Combination techniques (also *renrakuwaza*).
Ritsurei Standing bow.
Roku Six.
Ryo Ashi Dori Both ankles being held by Tori.
Ryote Two hands.
Ryu School – attached to most of the names of the Ju Jitsu system (*kito ryu*, etc.).

Sabaki Movement.
Saikatanden The lower abdomen.
San Three.
Sasai To support or prop.
Seisa All kneel together.
Seiza Correct sitting posture.
Sempai Senior student.
Senaka The back of the body.
Sensei Master or teacher.
Senshu A competitor or champion.
Seoi To carry on the back.
Seppuku The *bushi* method of committing suicide.
Shi Four.
Shiai Contest.
Shichi Seven.
Shihan Master, past master or *founder*.
Shiho Four quarters or four directions.
Shikko Knee walking.
Shime To tighten or strangle.
Shimewaza Techniques of neck-locking.
Shisei Posture.
Shita Below or underneath.
Shizentai Natural posture.
Shodan First degree.
Shomen Front of *dojo*, or top of head.
Shomen Uchi Straight downward attack to centre of head.
Sode Sleeve.
Sonemama Freeze, or stay where you are.
Soremade Stop, or that is all.
Soto Outside or outer.
Sukui To scoop up.
Sumi Corner.
Sutemi To throw away.
Sutemiwaza Techniques where Tori throws away his own body, sacrificing his posture.
Suwari Kneeling.
Suwariwaza Techniques performed with kneeling posture.

Tachi To stand, or sword.
Tachirei Standing bow.

Tachiwaza Techniques executed in standing position.
Tai Body.
Tani Valley.
Tanto Knife.
Tatami Judo mat.
Tate Vertical.
Te Hand.
Tegatana Handblade.
Toketa Broken.
Tokui Favourite *or* special.
Tomoe Turning over.
Tori The person who is throwing *or* who is executing the technique.
Towara A method of lifting where your arms are folded around from above and you throw an object over your head to your rear.
Tsugi Ashi A manner of walking in which one foot leads at each step and the other never passes it.
Tsuki Thrust *or* punch.
Tsukuri The action of breaking the opponent's balance.
Tsuri To fish up.

Uchi Strike.
Uchikomi A repetitive exercise where the throwing technique is taken to the point of *kate*.
Ude Arm.
Ue Above *or* on top of.
Uke The receiving player who is thrown.
Ukemi The breakfall.
Uki Floating.
Ura Back, rear *or* reverse.
Ushiro Behind *or* back of.
Utsuri Changing.

Wakare To divide *or* separate.
Waza Technique

Yama Mountain.
Yoko Side.
Yokomen Side of the head.
Yon Four.
Yoshi Carry on.
Yudansha Person holding back belt rank.

Zarei Formal kneeling bow.
Zazen Sitting meditation.
Zengo Forward and backward.
Zori Toe-grip straw sandals.

COUNTING IN JAPANESE

1 – *ichi* (ik)
2 – *ni*
3 – *san*
4 – *shi* or *yon*
5 – *go*
6 – *roku* (rok)
7 – *shichi* (ich)
8 – *hachi* (hash)
9 – *ku* (ker)
10 – *ju* (jer)

The words in brackets are (hopefully) the phonetic pronunciations of the numbers one to ten.

USEFUL PHRASES

Good morning – *Ohayo gozaimasu*
Good afternoon – *Konnichi wa*
Good evening – *Kondan wa*
Good night – *Oyasumi nasai*
Yes – *Hai*
No – *Iie*
Please – *Dozo*
Thanks – *Arrigato*
Thank you – *Domo arrigato*
Thank you very much – *Domo arrigato gozaimashita*
Let us begin – *Onegai shimasu*
I understand – *Wakarimasu* or *wakarimashita*
I don't understand – *Wakerimasen*

TO BEGIN THE SESSION

(1) Students stand at the edge of the mat in belt order.
(2) *Kioko* heels together.
(3) *Seisa* – all kneel together.
(4) *Rei wozuru* (if no Sensei is present) or *Sensei Zarei* – all students and instructors perform the kneeling bow except Sensei.
(5) If Sensei is present the senior belt on the mat then bows to Sensei who returns the bow.
(6) *Hui* – all stand up.

TO END THE SESSION

The ceremony is exactly the same as above. It is important that all students are correctly dressed with belts tied properly and knots in the centre. It is correct to end the session in the same manner as you began it.

INDEX
TO THE MAIN MOVEMENTS

GENERAL INDEX

FROM START TO END – FROM COLOUR TO COLOUR

The white is yours from the start,
*   so hold it well.*
Yellow, to eliminate your fear,
*   brings out the best.*
Orange, to feed the fruit of your labours,
*   to ban all pretext;*
Green, to gather wisdom like
*   Mother Earth.*
Blue, to reach for the sky
*   – its limits are yours.*
When Brown appears, like fertile soil,
*   you are almost settled.*
Only Black, at the last, helps you peer
through the darkness,
*   to the everlasting light of Arts.*

Dominick McCarthy